HISTORY OF OUR WORLD

ALL ABOUT THE UNIVERSE, HISTORY, AND LIFE ON OUR KNOWN WORLD

BHAGWATSHARAN GOYAL

ISBN 979-888591051-4

Vade Mēcum (Vah-dee Mee-khum] *n.* – Something regularly carried for frequent use or to reference, A book ready for reference, manual, handbook.

This book is a culmination of his lifework and passion for education. It will never cease to amaze you, at any turn, and open your eyes to wonders and marvels of our world. Originally hundreds of handwritten pieces of paper, I am proud to say this book has finally come to life, rendered beautifully according to 21st century technology. It is dedicated to him, my grandfather, Dr. Bhagwat Sharan Goyal. The Author.

Contents

Prologue

"...the World is Too Much with Us."

The world is too much with us; late and soon,
Getting and spending, we lay waste our powers; —
Little we see in Nature that is ours.
We have given our hearts away, a sordid boon!
This Sea that bares her bosom to the moon.
The winds that will be howling at all hours,
And are up-gathered now like sleeping flowers.
For this, for everything, we are out of tune.
It moves us not. Great God! I'd rather be
A Pagan suckled in a creed outworn.
So, might I, standing on this pleasant lea,
Have glimpses that would make me less forlorn.
Have sight of Proteus rising from the sea.
Or hear old Triton blow his wreathed horn.
William Wordsworth

God is great. World is wonderful. Nature is nice. Man is marvelous. During its known years of old history, mother earth has extended its bounties to all creatures, continents, and colossal bodies of water. Man's meticulous desire to survive and show its superiority over earth's elements has resulted in the creation of beautiful turnips on one side and discovery of nature's wonders on the other. This period has really sustained the interest of homo sapiens. Human efforts, combined with nature's gifts, have given life to today's tourisms. This culminates a better understanding of history and human instincts. Awe inspiring stars, solar systems, dinosaurs, and dragons have always caught the attention of the human imagination. This book is an effort to drive home the following ideas:

1. **As with Dinosaurs, all creatures, big or small, are part of grander schemes; they have their spots in history before history moves on.**
2. **Otherworldly bodies, like the solar systems, remind us that we are not alone and that other mysteries exist as well.**
3. **Although we claim to have explored all of mother earth, there are pitfalls in our knowledge.**
4. **The existence of our various flora and fauna is a miracle in itself.**
5. **Natural wonders present the great work nature, subsequently eliciting our respect and reverences.**

Consequently, the great personalities of our history have tried to solve the mysteries related to them. These endeavors developed civilization after civilization. Then, instinct to think freely and independently created religion, philosophy, literature. However, can we say that ambition, greed and pride corrupted man? No always so! Man's desire to live eternally (or be remembered all throughout time) has led to the creation of marvelous monuments. Old and modern monuments earn our appreciation for their creations; they are specimen of human intelligence, leaders, idols, and heroes. Evils and demons have been exposed through thousands of bloody wars and battles history presents us with. If evil and ambitious designs were responsible for ghastly wars and conquests, their creative nature presented a whole group of achievements in all fields, most notably architecture, arts, and sciences. Thus, decay and destruction have walked side by side of growth and grandeur: destruction becomes the greatest inspiration and stimulation for construction. Following destruction and chaos, humankind enters another period of peace and serenity. Works in the fields of art and literature spring up, subsiding the painful memories of death and destruction. Thus, the circle of life goes on with the march of mankind. This Is how I see the world, and what I have tried to capture within this book.

-B.S. Goyal

CHAPTER ONE

The Solar System

'Twinkle Twinkle little star': this immortal nursery rhythm always arouses the curiosity of children as well as elders concerning the universe that envelops them. The universe has been described as all the matter, energy and space that exists including: the sun, the planets, stars, galaxies, dust, and gas.

Planets revolve around stars, and billions of these make up galaxies. There are about 100 billion galaxies, which form separate clusters. Several clusters combine to make super clusters; these are the largest features of the universe. They are billions of light years away from each other. In 1998, the Keck 2 telescope in the Hawaii Island, the most powerful in the world, picked up light from a galaxy more than 12 billion light years away. Therefore, it can be guessed that the observable universe may extend up to 15 billion light years.

Birthing the universe:

About fifteen billion years ago, the entire universe was squashed into a very little, hot speck. It was too hot and full of energy to stay small. In a flash, it exploded outward. This event that gave birth to the universe is called the Big Bang. Neither space nor time existed before the Big Bang. However, both started when the universe began expanding. Since then, space has always been expanding, galaxies are constantly moving farther apart from each other. As time passed, the intense hot energy soup began cooling down. After millions of years, gas stars and galaxies were formed. Then about 10 billion years ago, our solar system and mother earth appeared.

Solar System:

In the solar system, there is one star (the sun), 9 planets, 63 moons, 6 big asteroids (at least 300 km in diameter), and many smaller asteroids, comets, and meteorites. Countless particles of dust and gas are floating between all these objects. The collision between asteroids, meteoroids and comets generate dust. Solar winds blowing outwards from the sun produces gas.

The Sun:

At the center of the Solar System, the sun's strong gravity holds the planets and keeps them from flying off into space. The sun is always traveling in space at speeds of 20 km per second. Its diameter is 1,392,000 km: in other words, it is 109 times the diameter of the Earth. Amazingly enough, the sun is the perfect star for the earth: it is just the right size and emits just the right amount of heat to sustain life on our planet. The sun is a very ordinary star if compared with other stars; there are other stars that are much larger and much hotter that it. The heat energy and light are created in the sun's core by a natural process called nuclear fusion, which creates enormous releases of tiny bits of light, called photons.

The temperature at the core is 15,000,000 Celsius and is 6000 Celsius on its surface. Photons take 10 billion years to travel from the core to the surface, but only eight minutes to travel from the surface to Earth, 150,000,000 km. Its mass is 2 million trillion kg, 330,000 times that of Earth. All the planets combined, including Earth, only make up 1% pf the mass of the sun. Its gravity is 28 times that of the Earths. It is 600,000 times brighter than a full moon. Its density is only .256 that of Earth, amazingly enough. It takes roughly 27 days (at the equator) for one rotation.

The sun vibrates and rings like a bell. The reason is its gas: it is made up entirely of gas, which is constantly blowing up and down. These fiery jets of gas leap to heights of 4000 km. All this movement causes vibrations, which in turn cause sound waves. The core of the sun is a gigantic nuclear furnace. Each second this fiery inferno transforms 700 million tons of hydrogen gas into helium gas through nuclear fusion. This sun is a gigantic magnet: it has the greatest pull at the equator, but a little les at the poles. This is because of its rotation. The uneven rotation strengthens the sun's magnetic fields. It is surprising that there are areas of cooler darker gas, called sunspots, on the sun's surface ranging from the width of a few hundred km – 80,000 km (which is about six times the Earth's diameter). These sunspots can last for months or even disappear after a day or two.

In constant evaporation, the Sun is losing charged gas particles. As they fly into space, they form the Solar Winds. As these Solar Wind particles zoom forward through space, they make up enormous speeds. By the time this wind reaches the Earth, it acquires a speed up to 750 km/s. The solar particles that hit the Earth's atmosphere cause geomagnetic storms. If the storm is very powerful, it can disrupt radio communications and interfere with the transmissions of electricity from plants. This was illustrated on March 10, 1989, when communication was lost with 11,000 of the 19, 00 satellites that were orbiting the Earth. Powerhouses had to be shut down in many parts of the Earth, for up to nine hours. About 1 million tons of particles, or Solar Plasma, rushed through coronal holes each second. Still the Sun has lost less than 0.1% of its mass since it was formed 4.6 bn years ago. As the Sun is the source of all life on Earth, almost all ancient civilizations worshipped it; Vedic cultures in Asia, Sumerians in Babylon, and Egyptians in Africa, Mayas and Incas in Americas were all Sun worshippers. They made huge temples to honor their deity.

Mercury:

Mercury is the first planet from the Sun. Its average distance from the Sun comes to 58 million km. It races through space, circling the Sun, once in 88 days. This is the shortest year (time taken to circle the Sun) in the Solar System. Still it rotates very slowly on its axis: it takes 59 days for one rotation (compared to Earth's 24 hours). As it is too near to the sun, it has the widest range of temperature on its surface: during the daytime it rises quickly to 400 C (a temperature hot enough to melt metals) and falls to -185 C at night. Its orbital speed (172,408 km/hr) makes Mercury the fastest planet. Because of its proximity to the Sun, the Sun's gravity pulls on it the hardest. Its diameter is 4,878 km.

Mercury has the one of the largest craters in the Solar System. It is called Caloris Basin. It was formed when a huge asteroid type of object slammed into it. The object hit so hard that it sent powerful shock waves throughout the planet. When the waves reached the other side of the planet, they shook and shattered the surface into a roughed-up area of hills and valleys. Mercury is like this because it does not have enough atmosphere to protect its surface against falling meteorites, asteroids, and comets. Comets, as a result, frequently smash into its surface. These craters make Mercury look very similar to Earth's Moon. Mercury's iron core makes up almost ¾ the size of the planet and is covered by layers of rock. When the core initially formed and cooled, it caused the planet's surface to wrinkle. This winkling caused huge cliffs to form across its bleak surface. The very thin layer of atmosphere which surrounds Mercury has only small traces of oxygen. Hence, there is no water. The atmosphere is too thin to carry sound or scatter light waves. Thus, Mercury is characterized by eerie silence and darkness during the day.

Venus

Venus is the second closest planet to the sun, with an average distance of 108 million km from it. Because of its density and size, it is referred to as "Earth's Twin". Venus was named after the Roman goddess of love and beauty. It is characterized as both a morning star and evening star. The diameter is 12,100 km and the mass are about 4/5 that of Earth. Venus has an atmosphere, but it is totally different from its twin. It is a hot inferno of poisonous gasses. The unbearable heat and pressure (90 times stronger than the Earths) is enough to turn lead to liquid. The atmospheric pressure is as great as being almost one kilometer under our ocean. The atmosphere is so thick that it always looks like a very cloudy day on Earth.

The sky is orange and casts a fiery glow over the ground below. This thick atmosphere makes the sunlight blend. That is why the sun looks strangely far and oval shaped from the planet. Venus's upper clouds race across the sky at speeds of 300 km/hr- three times as fast as most hurricanes on Earth. However, there aren't any winds on the surface. It is a boiling, barren desert. It does have a few towering mountains, some as high as 6 km. When the Russian space craft Venera 14 landed on Mercury in 1984, it could send back photos and data for only 57 minutes before it sizzled and melted.

It is a strange place; it is flatter than the Earth, and most of its surface is low like a rolling plane. On Venus, there are strangely shaped volcanoes. Groups of volcanoes have flattened, round domes which are 25 km across which look like pancakes. Some have domes shaped like giant spiders. These arachnid shaped volcanoes are called "Arachnoids". There are few meteorite craters on the surface. Most of its surface is presumed to be very young- about 400 million years old.

From the Earth, Venus looks beautiful, only the moon shines brighter in the night sky. The brightness is caused by its thick clouds, which reflect sunlight away from its surface. The clouds are filled with carbon dioxide, and other gases, that trap the heat- the greenhouse effect. Therefore, temperatures never drop below 500 Celsius- even at night. Both days and nights are very long on Venus, as it rotates only once every 243 days. Still, it revolves around the sun at orbital speeds of 126,111 km in 225 days. Thus, at Venus the day is longer than the year!

Earth

The Earth is often called the 'blue planet' because of the presence of its huge water bodies. It is the third planet from the sun, with an average distance of 150 million km. It rotates on its axis in 23 hours and 56 minutes, thus resulting in day and night. It also revolves around the sun, which takes 365.25 days. This makes up the year, resulting in the changing seasons. Its orbital speed is 107.245 km/hr. The diameter of the earth is 12,756 km, and its circumference is 40,000 km. The average surface temperature is 14 C. It has one moon which circles it.

The Earth is the most active of the rocky planets. Its surface is always changing. Its reason lies deep inside the planet. Its center, the core, is made of two hot layers of metal (one solid and one liquid) encased in a mantle of lava about 2800 km thick. The continental crust above the mantle is quite thin. Earth's crust is broken up into huge sheets called tectonic plates that ride on top of the gooey, elastic mantle. As these plates collide or pull apart from each other, the ground shakes and volcanoes erupt. As plates collide and subsequently weld together, the Earth's mountain rises and take shape. This process distorts the rock and compresses the sediments between two plates into mountains. The tallest mountains, the Himalayas, were formed in the same fashion from a body of water called 'Tethes'. For this reason, fish fossils have been found at the top of the mountains. There is a tremor- a shift in Earth's crust- every 30 seconds somewhere on the globe. The Pacific Ocean is rimmed with volcanoes. Mauna Loa, the largest volcanoes, has a height of 30,185 ft. and is in the Hawaiian Islands.

Apart from mountains, Earth consists of oceans (the Pacific is the largest with 70,015,000 sq. km.), rivers (the longest is the Nile, which stretched 4200 miles), canyons (the Grand Canyon, which is 445 km long, 1.6 km deep and 30 miles wide), deserts(the Sahara, which is 9,000,000 sq. miles), glaciers(the Hubbard glacier moving towards the ocean at 180 ft. per day), lakes (Baikal, the deepest), and above all rain (one inch of rain over an acre off ground leads to 102,747 liters of water). All the water on the Earth was produced during the planet's formation. It has been continuously recycled since then.

Life began on our planet about 3.5 billion years ago. The dinosaurs came along about 250 million years ago. Around the same time, the continents were joined into one large landmass called 'Pangaea'. Gradually, the continents began breaking apart and drifting away from each other. They continue to drift to this day. The first modern humans, the homo sapiens, came along 200,000 years ago.

Earth has many features which serve to distinguish it from the other planets. For starters, it is the only planet with so much water on its surface; water covers 2/3 of the planet's surface. The protective cover around it, the atmosphere, stops harmful ultraviolet rays from the sun from reaching the surface. This feature helps sustain life on the planet, making it the most singular and amazing unique characteristic of our planet.

Moon: The Earths Satellite

The moon has been the most lovable celestial body in folklore and literature. Poets all over the world has sung in its praise. On practical side, the moon is Earth's closest neighbor. The two have been traveling companions through space for more than 4 billion years. It orbits Earth due to the latter's gravity. Its average distance from Earth is 383,000 km and rotates on its axis in about 27 Earth days. It takes the same time in orbiting the Earth. The moon has a diameter of 3475 km-about ¼ of Earth's. Its mass and gravity are 1/81 and 1/6 of Earth's. This means that 45 kg on Earth weigh 7 kg on the moon. A long jumper can jump up to 120 feet on the moon if he jumps only 20 feet on our planet. The average surface temperature ranges from -160 C to 115 C.

The moon is a dead and hostile place. It has no gases and no atmosphere. Its surface is covered with craters which were caused by meteorites, asteroids, comets, and volcanos. About 3.5 billion years ago, lava flowed from the moon's interior and hardened into smooth plains called maria -the dark patches. Although the moon shines, it does not have any light of its own. It instead reflects the light from the sun. As it travels around the Earth, we see different aspects of it throughout the month. There changing aspect are called phases. The first phase is called 'New Moon', the second called 'Full Moon'. The Earth is then situated between the moon and the sun and the face of the moon that we see is completely lit up. The cycle of four phases is complete. This cycle lasts 29 days 12 hours and 44 minutes.

Tides on Earth are caused by the moon. The moon attracts water towards itself. Its gravity pulls the water directly below it, creating a bulge of water. At the time, the moon pulls the solid Earth away from the water on the opposite side of the Earth, creating a second bulge. As the moon moves around the Earth, these bulges of water follow it and move from east to west.

Man ventured into space for the first time over 50 years ago. The Russian Cosmonaut Yuri Gagarin was the first person to fly into space aboard the 'Vostok 1' on April 12, 1961. The sensational phase of space exploration culminated on July 21, 1969, when American astronaut Neil Armstrong set foot on the moon. After him, several men have walked on its surface and collected a total of 382 kg of rock samples for studies. The footprints left by these astronauts will remain on the moon for millions of years because the moon has no atmosphere: hence, no wind and no erosion. All these researches are evaporating the Romans of the moon.

Mars: The Red Planet

Mars is the red planet. Ancient people associated the planet with destruction. The Roman's gave this name to their god of war. Since then, scientists have used this name for the planet. The red color of Martian rocks might be linked to its high iron contents. It is the fourth planet from the sun with an average distance of 228 million km. It rotates once on its axis in 24 hours and 37 minutes. It takes 687 Earth days to revolve around the sun, with an orbital speed of 86,870 km/hour. Mars is the nearest planet to Earth. Therefore, mankind is heavily researching the planet. Its diameter, 6786 km, is slightly smaller than that of the Earth's. Its mass is 1/10 the Earth and gravity is 2/5 the Earth's. 45 kg on Earth would weigh 18 kg on Mars.

It has two moons, which circle around it. They are 'Phobos' and 'Deimos'. Both were probably asteroids that were caught within the gravitation pull of the planet. Phobos, the larger one, is closer to Mars and has a diameter of 28 km. It has a rocky surface with several craters including the huge Stickney crater, which covers 10% of its surface. Phobos circles the planet quickly: once every seven hours and 39 minutes. Deimos is only 16 km in diameter. It has a much smoother surface. It circles Mars once every 30 hours.

Mars and Earth have many things in common, enough to dub it Earth's younger brother. Length of one day is almost the same on both planets. Both have mountains, canyons, riverbeds, ice caps on the North Pole (which are dry on mars). The Viking probes have analyzed samples of the dusty surface but have been unable to identify any signs of insect life. However, the Mars Mission in 2004 has sent quite revealing pictures which suggest there might be fossils. The Chandrayan Mission of India (2008) has shown the presence of water. It also suggests that the conditions on the moon are much harsher than first expected. The atmosphere is extremely thin, with 95% carbon dioxide. There are violent winds that can reach speeds of hundreds of kilometers an hour. When this happens, they carry dust and turn into sandstorms, which can last several days. The sky looks rosy orange. Its icy winds can reach -50 C most of the times and have very little air.

Mars has some enormous features. One of them is the Marineris Valley, a system of canyons that runs for more than 4800 km added on to the size of the United States. There are also some enormous chasms. Another is called Olympus Mons, the largest volcano in the solar system. It is 600 km in diameter, 29 km high, and has a crater measure of 90 km across. This makes it almost three times as tall as the Earth's tallest land mountain- Mount Everest. It is 50 times more massive than the Earth's biggest volcano- Hawaii's Mauna Loa. Olympus Mons is extinct- that is, it stopped erupting long ago.

After the 2008 findings, possibilities have increased for landing man on the planet. Astronauts could ward off the extreme cold conditions by wearing especially designed space suits. Also, in the less than a decade, a space station called Freedom will make it easier for people to adjust for the weightlessness and make more mission to the planet.

Jupiter The Giant

Jupiter, the giant planet, derives its name from the king of gods worshipped by Romans. The colorful striped beach ball of a world is the biggest planet in the solar system. Its diameter is 139822 km. This is 11 times that of Earth. Jupiter is almost entirely made of gases. It has no solid surface. Instead, the planet has a small rocky core surrounded by immense layers of gas. These layers have been squeezed so hard by the planet's powerful gravity (2.5 times that of Earth) that they have turned solid and liquid. An outer atmosphere of gas, stretching about 70,000 km from the planet's center, gives way to stormy swirling layers of colors. Its surface is the most turbulent in the solar system. The colors seen on its surface are mostly yellow, red, brown, and purple. It would not be possible to land on Jupiter, as the surface under its clouds is not solid. Jupiter is mostly hydrogen and helium, just like the sun.

It is the fifth planet from the sun, with an average distance of 779 million km. It rotates on its axis very fast: about ten hours. The revolution around the sun is 12 Earth years, with a speed of 47,043 km an hour. It's very cold, with the average temperature remaining at -43 C. Jupiter is the most massive planet in the solar system. It is 318 times more massive than the Earth. In fact, its mass is 2.5 that of all other planets combined. All the other planets and moons could evenly fit inside Jupiter. Only Saturn comes close in size and it would occupy just more than half of Jupiter's volume. Even Jupiter's solid core has three times the volume of Earth's.

Fierce storms and enormous banks of clouds are always moving through Jupiter's atmosphere. The largest of these storms- largest of any planet- is the Great Red Spot. It is Jupiter's most visible feature. Today, it measures about 25,000 km x 50,000 km. It spins around its center every six days and has been raging for more than 350 years. The light oval just beneath it is a smaller storm that formed only 50 years ago.

Jupiter has 16 moons. They spread out across more than 23 million km of space. Four of them were discovered by Galileo on January 17, 1610- Lo, Europa, Ganymede and Callisto, are about the size of Earth's moon. The other 12 are tiny, with Leda merely ten km in diameter. Lo has active volcanoes. It was the first time, in 1990, the Magellan space probe found such things anywhere other than the Earth. Lo's volcano spews out sulfur instead of lava. The ground is yellow and orange with sulfur and salt. Calisto is covered with craters. Some of its volcanoes may still be active. They throw out ice and water, which probably freeze. It has more craters than any other object in its solar system.

Saturn: Ringed Planet

Saturn, named after the Roman god of harvest, is the second largest planet and sixth planet from the sun. Its distance from the sun is 1.43 billion km. This makes it the farthest planet to be seen through naked eyes. It has seven major bands containing thousands of ringlets. One of the rings can be seen through a simple telescope. Other planets, including Jupiter, also have rings. However, they are not as spectacular as that of Saturn.

Saturn is also a gas giant, like Jupiter. It gives of more energy than it gets from the sun. It is one of the four giant planets composed of gas and ice (the other three are Jupiter, Neptune, and Uranus). Made up of low-density matter, hydrogen, helium, and methane gases, it is so light that it could have floated if it were on a huge ocean. The planet has a hot rocky core surrounded by liquid and solid gases. The outer layer is made of gases and clouds. The average temperature at cloud tops remain at -185 C.

Also, like Jupiter, Saturn spins at a dizzying speed and completes one rotation on its axis in 10.7 hours. The fast spinning craters bulge around its equator, where its diameter (116489 km) makes it nine times bigger than the Earth. It completes one revolution around the Sun in about 29 Earth days with an orbital speed of 34,703 km/hr. Its mass is 95 times and gravity 1.1 times that of Earth. A 45 kg object on Earth would weigh 50 kg. on Saturn.

Because of its rapid rotation, there are strong winds in its atmosphere. They race along at up to 1500 km/hr-four times faster than the fastest tornado on Earth. Several very thin rings revolve around the planet, about its equator, and spread out over a great distance. The rings are made up of millions of dust particles encased in ice which orbit the planet. The particles are thought to be the remains of a shattered moon. These pieces are slowly falling back onto the planet and will disappear within 100 million years unless another moon breaks up and forms new rings. A few years ago, Voyager 2 sent pictures of Saturn. This revealed that there are thousands of rings with different chemicals inside of them. They are amazing complexes.

Saturn has the largest number of moons-18. Pan is the smallest, merely 19 km in diameter. The closest moon, Phoebe, is probably a captured asteroid or comet. Titan, the largest of Saturn's companions, is the second biggest moon in the solar system. It measures 5,150 km across. It is the only one with a thick atmosphere-thicker than that of the sun. In Hindu mythology, Saturn is the most feared god because of his temper. Therefore, he is worshipped. To astronomers, it is just a huge lump of gases.

Uranus: The Sideways Green Planet

One of the giant planets, Uranus is four times the size of the Earth. It is the seventh from the sun, with an average distance of 2.86 billion km. It is the second largest planet, with a 50,724 km diameter and a mass of 14.5 times that of the Earth. In gravity, it has only 9/10 pull as that of Earth. A 45 kg object on Earth would weigh 41 kg on the planet. It has a day of 17 hours. Being very far from the sun, to takes 80 Earth years to orbit the sun. Its orbital speed 24, 506 km/hr. The season on Uranus are quite odd, due to the axitial tilt of 97.9 degrees. One pole of the planet points directly at the sun during that poll's midsummer. 42 years later-half a year for Uranus- the other pole points at the sun. Therefore, it is warmer at the polls than at the equator.

Photos taken by the Hubble space telescope show that the picture was turned sideways. Its rings and moons are all flipped on their side. No one is sure why Uranus is tilted like this. It may have smashed into an Earth sized object early in its history. This could have knocked it on its side and chipped off the debris that forms its moon and rings.

Uranus is classified as a gas giant. Methane in the planet's atmosphere gives it a blue-green color. It was first discovered in 1690 through a telescope. Hydrogen, helium, steam, and methane compose its atmosphere. The temperature varies between 150 C and -220 C. Much of the planet's interior is liquid, or a hot slushie mixture of water and gases. This liquid surrounds a rocky core.

In addition to its 10 dark rings, Uranus also has 17 moons. 12 have been discovered, all after 1986. They are all less than 1600 km wide. Most are named after characters in the plays of William Shakespeare. Their true sizes and distances are not yet known. Titania, 14 from the planet, is probably the biggest. Cordelia is the closest and the smallest of all moons. Mirayd, the 11, is the most interesting. It is the fifth largest moon and has a surface unlike that of any other moon or planet. Lightly cratered areas sit next to grooved places coronae. No one knows what produced such a varied landscape.

Uranus is barren and icy. It has no atmosphere. The ground is rough, rugged, and jagged. Huge ridges and valleys lead to giant cliffs twice the height of Mount Everest. In the moon's dark sky, Uranus grows huge and blue green against a background of glittering stars. Uranus is named after the roman god of heaven.

Neptune: A Windy Planet

Neptune is the last of the giant planets. Voyager 2, after a journey of 12 years, finally reached Neptune in 1989. It has been named after the roman god of the sea. It is the coldest of all the giant gas planets. Its distance of 4.49 billion km from the sun and eighth position makes it so. It is also the windiest planet. Along its equator, Neptune's winds race eastward at speeds greater than 2000 km/hr. Neptune also gives off more heat than it gets from the sun. Heat rising from within the planet moves through the atmosphere in currents. The currents are twisted by Neptune's rapid wind, creating strong winds. The colder the planet, the more violent the winds are. Thus, the average temperature at cloud tops remains -225 C.

A day on Neptune lasts about 16 Earth hours, and its revolution around the Sun takes 164 Earth years with an orbital speed of 19,524 km/hr. Its diameter of 49,526 km makes it the fourth largest planet in the solar system. Its mass is 17.1 times and gravity are 1.1 times that of Earth's. Neptune's winds power is enormous storms. Four large oval storms were detected by Voyager 2. The biggest, named 'The Great Dark Spot' is accompanied by bright cloud features, nicknamed Scooter. Wispy clouds, looking like Earth's cirrus clouds change rapidly on the planet, forming and disappearing over several hours. It has four dusty rings, which are much thicker in some places than others.

Freezing clouds, tinted by methane, give Neptune its blue color. It has eight moons. Except for Triton, all are relatively small. Narold has a weird orbit: it comes as close as 1.4 km close to Neptune and takes it as far as 9.6 million km away. Triton is a giant of a moon- the largest body in the solar system to orbit backward. Its path around Neptune is tilted relative to the planet's equator. Perhaps Triton is a captured small planet. It will slowly spiral inwards in its backward orbit, dooming it to crash into Neptune within the next 100 billion years. At -225 C, the surface of triton is the coldest in the solar system. Nitrogen and Methane ice cover everything, giving the moon a blue tint. Huge geysers spew nitrogen, ice, and carbon compounds high into Triton's thin atmosphere. There might be enormous frozen lakes and wrinkled terrain.

Pluto: The Ice Planet

Pluto was discovered in 1930. It is the smallest planet in the solar system, about the size of Earth's moon. The diameter is 2274 km. It is invisible to the naked eyes. Light reflected from the surface takes 5 hours and 2 minutes to reach us. It is the farthest planet from the sun: 5.9 billion km away. It gets very little sunlight. We know very little about Pluto, as none of the space crafts have ever visited it yet. One rotation on its axis (which is tilted 98.3 degrees) takes six Earth days. One revolution around the sun takes 240 Earth years, at an orbital speed of 17,091 km/hr. Pluto's mass is only 1/45 times the Earth. It has little gravity in comparison with the Earth: 7/100. A 45 kg object on Earth would weight 3 kg on Pluto.

It is believed that it has a thin frigid atmosphere of methane and nitrogen that is slowly escaping into space. The temperature of the surface remains between -228 C and -238 C. When Pluto reaches its closest point to the sun, the atmosphere is gas. When it moves away from the sun, the atmosphere is transformed into a snowy layer on the surface. We also know that Pluto's polls are tipped nearly 99 degrees relative to its orbit.

Of all the planets, Pluto has the most eccentric orbit. For 20 years (out of each 20-48), Pluto's orbit lay inside Neptune. This last occurred from 1977 to 1999. Pluto's tilted path also takes it far above the other planets when it is farthest from the sun.

In 1978, astronomer James Christi of the US Navy observatory discovered that Pluto has a moon: Charon. It is half the size of Pluto, and it orbits very close to the planet. Its orbit is tilted so steeply that it swings above and below Pluto's orbit around the sun. Astronomers sometimes think of these two small companions as a double planet. Charon appears bluer than Pluto. Charon's surface has never been seen. Scientists believe it's a desolate world, covered with hills of water and ice. One side of the moon always faces Pluto, which hangs in the starry sky like a frozen twin. Very little warmth reaches Charon, and the sun looks like a bright far away star. It is always night on Charon. Because Pluto is such a foreboding world, it takes its name from the roman god of the dead.

There has been talk over the last decade to take Pluto out of the list of planets, due to its small size. In the 2009 Geographical Summit, this matter was raised. Scientists were not unanimous on this matter. Hence, Pluto remains the ninth planet.

Asteroids: Minor Member 1

Asteroids mean "star like" in Greek. About 200 years ago, they were unknown. When astronomers started looking for a missing planet between Mars and Jupiter, they fell upon innumerable rocks of various sizes circling the sun. They named these rocks asteroids. The biggest of them, Ceres, was the first to be discovered. Its discoverer, Giuseppe Piazzi, named it after the goddess of agriculture. It has a diameter of 913 km. Astronomers believe that there might be 1 million asteroids in the solar system. Asteroids are in the habit of colliding with one another in their path around the sun. All of them are made up of solid materials, like rocks and metals.

They have been divided into about a dozen different types. There are three main types though. The 'C'type is blackish in color, containing a lot of carbon. This type of asteroid does not reflect the sunlight well. It remains the darkest. It includes Davida. Such asteroids are found in the outer region of the Asteroid Belt. The second, 'M' type, such Psyche, are made of metals like nickel and iron. They are found in the middle region. Often silvery grey, they are the brightest. 'S' type is the third. They are reddish in color, and contain a rocky material called Silicate. It is just like beach sand. Euronnia is an example of an M type asteroid. They live within the inner region of the asteroid belt. They take 3-6 years to make one orbit around the sun.

Comets: Minor Member 2

A comet is a ball of ice and dust surrounded by a cloud of gas and dust. As it approaches the sun, the heat causes the ice in the core to evaporate into gas. They gave earned the nick name 'Dirty Snowballs'. The gas and dust glow, as they reflect the sunlight forming a long tail. Many comets have tails that stretch for millions of km. Most of them come from the farthest, coldest reaches of the solar system.

They are satellite of the sun and have orbits in the shape of a long narrow ellipse. They are the only object able to travel as far as, and beyond, Neptune and Pluto. Some swing around the sun every 200-300 years. Others have orbits which bring them closer to the sun and Earth: only once in hundreds and thousands of millions of years sometimes. Each time a comet passes close to the sun, it loses some of its mass. Eventually, so much has gone that it no longer grows. It then becomes a small dark asteroid. Although some comets are visible to the naked eye, they can usually be seen only in telescopes.

The famous Haley's Comet was seen first in 1910, then in 1986. It has been appearing after every 76 years since at least 246 BC. The comet 'Hillbop' was one of the brightest in living memory. It came no closer than 190 million km to the surface. We will not see this comet again for another 2380 years.

The appearance of comets has always been viewed with suspicion and fear: it was regarded as a bad omen. Many terrible events, such as the defeat of Attila the Hun, assassination of Julius Caesar, downfall of Montezuma, several droughts, and plagues, have been attributed to the appearance of comets.

Meteorites: Minor Member Number 3

These are the dusty remains of comets, or chips of asteroids. Every day, millions of bits of cosmic debris hurl through Earth's atmosphere. They range from microscopic dirt particles to rock several kg in weight. It is estimated that during the year, 400000 tons of material rain down on the Earth. Only 1/10 of these particles reach the ground. Most burn up in the atmosphere. These are classified as meteorites until the ground. If they burn up in a streak of light before reaching the ground, they are called 'meteors. A very bright meteor is called a fireball.

It is very rare to see a meteorite hitting the earth. On the evening of October 9, 1992, Michelle Knapp of Peekskill New York heard a meteorite crash. The football-sized space rock crushed the trunk of her car, as it sat in her driveway. The world's largest known meteorite, called Hoba, was discovered in 1920 on a farm in Namibia. This 65-ton boulder fell to the Earth in prehistoric times. It is about 3 meters long, and 2.5 meters wide. It has not been moved.

If big, they can produce a giant impact on the Earth. These gigantic space bombs create spectacular flashes of light as they rocket through the atmosphere at speeds up to 50 km/sec. When they hit the Earth, they can create huge craters. Scientists believe that huge meteorites were the cause of about 100 gigantic craters around the Earth. The largest is Chicxulub basin, centered in the Mexican Yucatan peninsula. It has a diameter of about 300 km. The Berringer Meteor crater in Arizona was found when a 3000-ton meteorite hit the Earth (50,000 years ago). It is 168 meters deep, and 1200 meters wide. Many scientists believed that the dinosaurs were killed when a comet or asteroid collided with the Earth 65 million years ago. On June 30, 1908, a powerful meteorite exploded in midair and instantly flattened trees up to 18 km in Tunguska, a remote area in Russia.

Mother Earth

The Earth is the most unique planet in the whole universe as it supports life. For a long time, it was thought that the earth is only about 4,500 years old. The Christians came to this conclusion by combining the ages of all the people mentioned in the Bible from Adam and Eve to Jesus Christ. With the discovery of fossils of the extinct animals in the 19th century it became quite clear that the earth must have been much, much older. Now it is with new findings in the solar system itself the earth has come to be as old as 4.6 billion years. In this system our earth fits in the middle so far as size is concerned. It is ten times the size of Mercury, the smallest planet, but thirteen hundred times smaller than Jupiter, the biggest of all.

It's center (core) is made of two hot layers of metals-one molten and other solid, encased in a metal of lava about 2,800 km thick. The continental shelf above this metal is quite thin (only 70 km). The outer core of the molten metal is 2,000 km thick with a temperature of 2,200-degree C. The inner solid core is 900 km thick and has a temperature of 4,500-degree C. This core is solid due to pressure. The earth's magnetic field is caused by the rotation of the inner core.

Some 150 million years ago there was only one huge landmass Pangaea amidst one enormous Panthalassa. This land mass broke apart some 152 million years ago and the pieces drifted apart slowly and reached their present position. The study of the globe shows that the continents fit together like pieces of a jigsaw puzzle. These continents are drifting apart even now. North and South America continue to drift away from Eurasia at the rate of 4 centimeters per year. At the same time, India is moving into Asia at 5 centimeters per year. This is causing the increase of one centimeter in the height of Mt. Everest every year. Africa is drifting north and might squeeze the Mediterranean Sea to a channel. East Africa will split off from the main continent due to the drift valley, creating a new ocean. But all this will happen in the next 150 million years.

About two billion years ago, a thick coating of water covered most of this rocky surface. The forces generated by the rising currents of heat inside caused the surface to break into mosaics of huge slowly creeping land mass called tectonic plates. There are 20 in number and are still on the move. In some zones these plates move apart but in some they collide. One of the plates descends below the other into the magma, creating trenches. The plate that moves up form's mountains or volcanoes. Sometimes when they collide great natural calamities like earthquakes occur.

Geographically the whole land mass is divided into seven continents- Asia, Africa, North America, South America, Europe, Australia, and Antarctica. These continents are further divided into more than two hundred countries except Antarctica, all the continents have water bodies, mountains, volcanoes, deserts, forests, flora and fauna, cities and agricultural land to support more than 6 billion population and other forms of life. Natural calamities- earthquakes, hurricanes, tornadoes, lightening etc. also hit the continents. All these features not only make the Earth a complex planet but the liveliest one.

Oceans:

From the outer space the plant looks entirely blue. It's because more than 2/3 of the space is occupied by ocean waters. These ocean waters have been divided into four separate oceans that is the Atlantic, Pacific, Indian, and the Arctic Ocean.

The Pacific Ocean is the biggest ocean of all. It has a surface area of 180 million square km and accounts for half of the total ocean water. It is bigger than all the continents put together. It is the deepest of all. It conceals abysses up to eleven km deep. The highest mountains could easily fit inside an abyss. The deepest spot is near the island of Guam in Marina Trench. A unique marine animal life has developed in this abyss. The largest volcano Mauna Loa, higher than Mt. Everest, lies in its bottom near the Hawaiian Islands. Its rim from America to Asia is packed with volcanoes. Several them are still active. The deeper pacific contains about 50 times more water than the Arctic.

The Atlantic Ocean separates the American continents from Africa and Europe. It has an area of 94,310,000 square km. It appeared late (about 100 million years ago) when the continents moved apart. It covers roughly 20% of the earth's surface. Being the second largest ocean, it occupies an elongated "S" shaped basin extending in a North-South direction and is divided into North Atlantic and South Atlantic by equatorial counter currents at about 8-degree north latitude. An average depth is 3,322 meters. The greatest depth 8,605 meters is in Puerto Rico Trench. At the bottom there is a great submarine mountain range called Mid-Atlantic Ridge. A great rift valley also extends along the Ridge over most of its length. The salinity of the surface waters in the open ocean ranges from 33-37 parts per thousand but varies with latitudes and seasons.

The ocean has also contributed significantly to the development and economy of the countries around. All the famous sailors, Vikings, Christopher Columbus, Vasco De Gama, Magellan, and Frances Drake spent years on its waters. It offers abundant petroleum deposits and world's richest fishing resources. The Indian Ocean has an area of 7,402 square km. It is the third largest ocean. It has been named after India which makes its northern boundaries. The whole eastern coast of Africa, Northern Antarctica, and Western Australia lie on its shorelines. The northeastern part of the ocean is the deepest. Here the greatest known depth is 8,000 meters.

The chief arms of the Indian Ocean are the Arabian Sea and the Bay of Bengal. Along the coast of India, Asia and Africa, several large rivers empty into the Indian Ocean. They include, the Indus, the Brahmaputra, the Irrawaddy, the Salween, the Ganges, the Shatal-Arab (Tigris and Euphrates) and the Zambezi. The chief islands in the ocean are Madagascar, Mauricious, Ceylon, and Reunion. The Suez Canal connects it to the Mediterranean Sea and thus it becomes a hub of maritime activities. On the far eastern side, Singapore is its gateway, hence a very strategic place. All the trade with the East was done through this ocean as the winds are usually gentle. But hurricanes sometimes sweep in, especially in the Bay of Bengal. It is the only source of monsoons in India and adjoining countries.

The Arctic Ocean is the smallest in the area (12,260,000 square km). It contains a ridge that is one thousand meters below the surface which is covered by ice. It divides the ocean into two basins, the Laurentian and Angara. The Angara basin reaches a depth of 4,087 meters. Closest to the North Pole, when it is very deep below the ice, the North Pole is the middle of the icy Arctic. This remains frozen for most of the year. It is surrounded by the land mass of Europe, Asia, North America, and Greenland. It is connected to the Pacific Ocean by the Bering Strait and to the Atlantic through Greenland Sea. The greatest inflow of water comes from the Atlantic via Norwegian currents. Water also enters from the Pacific via Bering Strait. It is the major source of cold air that inevitably moves towards the equator meeting the warmer air in the middle latitudes and causing rain and snow. The Arctic Ocean is strategically important as the shortest route between North America and Russia.

Mountains:

When the two continental plates meet, a mountain appears. It takes 50-100 million years for a mountain to rise. Mountain chains are composed of faults or cracks and intrusions of many complex rocks. The Alps in Europe are the result of collision of Europe and northern Italy with the African Plate. The formation took 40 million years. The Himalayas were formed when a huge island, India, collided with the landmass of China. Mt Kilimanjaro in Africa is a volcano. The effect of frost, winds, and rain gives mountains their sharp peaks. The Himalayas are the world's highest mountains. It has 14 peaks over 8,000 meters. Everest, K2 Kanchenjunga top others. In comparison to them, the peaks in other continents are lower; Aconcagua (Argentina, South America) is 6,959 meters, Mt. McKinley (Alaska, North America) is 6,194 meters, Mt. Kilimanjaro (Tanzania, Africa) is 5,895 meters, and Elbrus (Russia, Europe) is only 5,642 meters. High in the mountains the air is thinner, and oxygen is low. This air cannot hold heat and water very well. Thus, the temperature drops drastically after the sunset. Few animals and plants can survive in this harsh environment.

Volcanoes also appear where plates either move apart or collide and rub against each other. As they collide, small cracks appear, and molten rock comes to the surface; this is the first eruption. The shape of the volcano depends on the eruption itself-the way lava comes out and hardens on the volcanoes' surface. They are still appearing. In Japan, a volcano suddenly appeared in the middle of a village lifting it by 100 meters. Most of the volcanoes are near the seacoasts and at the bottom of the sea that is on the edge of the continental plates. The chief region is around the Pacific Rim and Southern Indonesia. Tristan Da Cunha, the Azores and the Canaries in the Atlantic. The Mt. Kilimanjaro was formed in the middle of Africa rift.

There are two types of volcanoes on the earth. One extinct, which have not erupted in the last 10,000 years such as Mt. Kilimanjaro, and the second, active which can erupt any time. There are about 1,400 different volcanoes in the world. But only eight countries share 865 of them, Russia tops with 171 follows by Indonesia with 161. When a volcano erupts it causes a great loss of life, property, and land. Mt. Pinatubo, Philippines erupted in June 1991. A timely warning saved 250,000 people but 800 lost their lives. On May 8th, 1980, Mt. St. Helens in Washington State of the USA erupted with the fury of 500 atomic bombs. An avalanche of a stony debris was overtaken by a wave of scalding hot gases and choking ash. Timely warnings saved all lives except 61. The biggest eruption was caused in 1815 when Indonesia's Mt. Tambura killed 12,000 people outright and another 80,000 by starvation and disease. The other notorious eruptions were Vesuvius, Italy in A.D. 79 and Krakatau, Indonesia in 1883. It is that tens of thousands of lives were lost. Recently in April 2010 a volcanic eruption in Iceland disrupted the flights in Europe.

Deserts:

Deserts are vast, dry land regions on the earth. They cover about 1/5 of the surface of land and are found on all the continents. They don't have to be scorching hot. They might be the coldest regions like Antarctica, Gobi or Tibet were the temperature stays below 0 degrees C. They don't have to be sandy either as 85% of the world's deserts don't have sand dunes. One thing is common, that they are the driest places where almost no vegetation can sustain its growth. None of the deserts get more than 25 centimeters of rain in a year.

Almost all the deserts are too far from the sea. The largest and the emptiest is the continent of Antarctica, with an area of 14,000,000 square km. The whole continent is covered with a thick layer of ice. At the South Pole, it is 4 km thick. These icy deserts contain water, but it is frozen. The Gobi Desert in central Asia in the western China stretches for an area six times larger than that of the United Kingdom, the driest place in the area and Tibet in the Himalayas at the altitude of 4,880 meters are far from the sea. But the word desert is tagged with the mighty Sahara of North Africa which measures 5,150 km from east to west and 2,250 km from north to south. It is famous for its dunes. Here the temperature in the day reaches 45 degrees C but drops at night to 0 degrees C. High winds in the day transfers the entire landscape. The Atacama Desert in Northern Chile, South America is the driest desert. It has less than 1.3 centimeters of rain in a year. Similarly, the Kalahari Desert between Zambezi River in southern Africa has a vast area of 500, 0000 square km is the world's largest continuous expense of sand.

In Europe, Spain has the desert landscaping. Arid conditions and soil erosion have affected the province of Almeria in the south of Andalusia. In North America, the monumental valley of Arizona, Mohave, the red sand, and stone desert stretching from Arizona to Utah provide rugged and desolate looks. Despite dryness, deserts provide date, the sweetest of the fruits. Some of the liveliest cities such as Teheran (Iran) and Las Vegas (USA) are situated in the deserts.

Forests:

Forests cover about 20% of the lands surface of the earth. Inside the forests it is moist and cool. These temperate and cool forests are found on all the continents except Antarctica. They need more than 750 millimeters of rain per year. They block most of the wind, making a forest a stable environment for plants and animals to grow. There may be broad-leaf trees where the climate is mild and wet or mixed trees broad-levered and conifers in colder regions. There are evergreen, oak, beech, ash, birch, among the broad-leaf trees and pine, firs, cedars, and spruce in conifers. Many species such as elk (the largest type of deer), wolverine, and panda are found.

Then there are rainforests. They are called dark jingles also. They are found near the equator where the climate is warm and wet. These forests get an average 2,000 millimeters of rain each year. The combination of abundant sunlight and plenty of rain has produced a diverse range of plants and animals. They are home to more than have of the plant and animal species in the world. The rubber tree, cacao bean plants, the copaiba which provide a substitute of diesel are a rare species of trees. One can see toads to tigers and colorful birds in the forests.

The third important forest are savannah. They are open grasslands in Africa. They trees are much smaller. Here the dry season is followed by the rainy season and the vegetation is capable of surviving both the extremes. High grass, thorny acacia trees and the famous baobabs provide shelter and support for herbivore animals such as elephants, giraffes, buffalos, zebras, gazelle, rhinoceros and carnivores like lions, hyenas, cheetahs etc. Many species of birds such as flamingos, herons and ibises also find them conducive. Forests are the lifeline of the earth because they provide everything that the earth needs for survival.

Apart from the above-mentioned features, the human habitation has also become complicated. About 250 years ago most of the population lived in villages in small groups. They were almost self-sufficient, but the scientific inventions and increased trade brought about the development of cities, metropolitans, and now super cities with the population of over 10 million people. Mexico City and Tokyo are packed with almost 20 million people each. London, Bombay, Delhi, and Shanghai are crossing 15 million each and New York, Cairo, and Lagos have already crossed the 10 million mark. At least 30 cities around the world have more than 5 million people. This urbanization is increasing its own problems, but they have become the hub of all activities in the world. The world's population is growing very fast: about 6 billion people have greeted the 21st century. Some continents have become more crowded than others and have different population rates (the fastest in Africa and Latin America).

Continents:

North America: This continent is made up of ten countries. The largest three are the USA, Canada, and Mexico. The other seven lie in south of Mexico. This continent also includes the biggest island called Greenland. It is believed that the first human habitation on this continent started about 16,000 years ago. The early settlers probably came from Asia crossing Alaska through the land bridge Berengia that once joined the two continents over Bering Strait. They migrated traveling as far as South America. The area of the continent is 9,366,000 square km and the population is 470,000,000. The US and Mexico are the most populated with 290 million and 98 million people respectively. Mexico City with 20 million, which is the most populated one followed by New York (18,054,000 people) and Los Angeles (13,471,000 people). Mississippi-Missouri (USA) with 6,019 km and Mackenzie are the largest rivers. Mt. McKinley (Denali), US (6,194 meters) and Mt. Logan, Canada (5,951 meters) are the highest mountains.

South America: It is the fourth largest contingent on the earth with an area of 17,819,000 square km. Although this continent has mountains, forests, plains, and deserts, it is dominated by two geographic features: Andes Mountain and the Amazon River. The Andes are the longest chain of mountains in the world as they run an entire length of the continent on the western side. The Amazon cuts across the continent through Brazil's Amazon

Basin, the world's largest rainforest. Today it is made up of twelve countries- Brazil, Argentina, and Peru being the largest. The climate changes drastically from hot tropical in the North to the freezing cooler regions in the South where it nearly touches Antarctica. The population has reached 332,000,000 and it's multiplying rapidly. Brazil and Argentina with 162,000,000 and 36,000,000 people are the most populous countries. Amongst cities Sao Paulo (15,784,888) and Rio De Janeiro (10,489,000) in Brazil and Buenos Aires (9,988,000), Argentina are leaders. The highest mountains are Aconcagua (6,960 meters), Ojos Del Salado (6,908 meters) and Bonete (6872 meters). Amazon (6437 km), Parana (4,500 km) and Madeira (3,200 km) can claim to be the longest rivers on the continent.

Europe: It is a small but the most scenic continent. It is the jagged eastern end of the huge land mass called Eurasia. It is less than half the size of North America (10,530,750 square km). But it is densely populated (728,000,000 people). No part of the Western Europe is more than 480 km from the sea. That is why fishing and sailing played a great in its development and making it a ruler of the world. The oldest cities of the world Athens (Greece), Rome (Italy), Vienna (Austria), Paris (France), and London (England) came up on the banks of rivers. The mountains- The Pyrenees, the Alps, the Caucasus, and the Balkans- kept people isolated so they developed different cultures and some 40 languages, resulting in 42 countries. The most populous countries include European-Russia (147,000,000) and Germany (82,000,000). Vatican with only 830 people is the smallest country in the world. The biggest cities are London (11,000,000), Moscow (9,390,000) and Paris (8,510,000). The Volga (3,531 km), the Danube (2,858 km), The Ural (2,400 km) are the longest rivers in Europe. It has 80,000 km of coastline which helps greatly in trade and traffic. Lately the people of Europe are trying to unite themselves under the European community. Presently it has 27 countries with the Euro as a common currency.

Asia: This is the biggest continent with an area of 4457900 square km and a population of 3,604,000,000. It is a land of extremes. There are 46 countries (most populous is China- 1,249,200,000- and India-1,057,000,000). Asia takes up nearly 1/3 of the Earth's land surface. It stretches from the North above the Arctic Circle to south below the equator and east from the Ural Mountains and the Caspian Sea to within 88 km of Alaska's Seaward Peninsula of North America. There are vast deserts that cover the Arabian Peninsula, sections of China and central Asia. But there are worse densest forests in Southeast Asia. It is the home of valuable natural resources. Most of the people still live in a traditional life but all the countries are developing them on modern lines. All the world's religions were born in Asia. Hence the largest number of places of pilgrimage. The highest mountain range of the world, The Himalayas, with 14 peaks above 8,000 meters reigns supreme with Mt. Everest (8,848 meters) and Mt. K2 (8,611 meters). Asia has the lowest point of the world also in the Dead Sea. It is 408 meters below the sea level. Its longest rivers are Yangzi, China (6,380 km) and Brahmaputra, India. Mawsyram, India is the wettest place in the world with an average rainfall of 11,873 millimeters. Singapore is the most densely populated country with 5,654 people per square km. But the least populated country also lies in Asia, which is Mongolia with only 1.5 people per square km. The most populated metropolitan areas are Tokyo (27,242,000), Bombay (15,725,000) and Shanghai (13,659,000).

Africa: This is the second largest continent with an area of 30,065,000 square km. It spreads across more than 1/5 of the earth's land surface. The world's largest, hot desert the Sahara (35,000,000 km), the longest river, the Nile (6,825 km), a wide band of tropical rainforests, volcanoes, and many of the world's most unusual animals and plants are in Africa. There has been a very little difference during the last 500 million years. The earliest human remains (Olduvai Gorge and 3.6-million-year-old footprints near Laetoli, Tanzania) and the oldest land mass exist in Africa. The population of this vast continent is much less than that of Europe (6,546,000,000 people). There are more than 50 countries and hundreds of different languages. Famous early civilizations (Egypt 3,000 B.C., Ghana 500 A.D., Zimbabwe 1,000 A.D., and Sungari, Mali, and Niger 1,400 A.D.) had flourished here. Among natural features Mt. Kilimanjaro, Tanzania (5,895 meters) presents a scenic view. Natural wonders- Ngoro Ngoro Crater, Serengeti, Tsavo, and Croggar game parks, Rift Valley, and the largest island Madagascar (587,000 square km), the fourth largest island in the world- all add to its natural diversity. European powers ruled much of Africa in 19th century, adding settlers and their customs to Africa's rich mix. The vibrant diverse cultures that have developed in Africa reflect the importance of its natural resources including gold and diamond. Its largest cities are Lagos (10,878,000), Nigeria, Cairo (10,000,000). The world' s hottest place Dallol (average temperature 34 degrees C), Ethiopia and the lowest point Lake Asal (156 m below sea level) Djibouti, of Somalia, all lie in Africa.

Australia: The biggest island is the only country that consists of the whole continent (area 7682300 sq km). It is the least populated (18700000 people) with least density (2.3 people per km) in the world. Being a great island, it has no borders with any other country. It takes its name from a Latin word 'Australis' which means 'Southern'. Since Australia lies to the south of the equator it has been named as such. It is divided into six states- including the island of Tasmania and two territories. All major cities except the capital Canberra are situated along the coast. 54% of the population lives in four big cities- Sidney (3600000), Melbourne (3100000), Brisbane (1300000) and Port Harcourt (1100000). Darling is the longest river with a length of 2739 km, Central part of the continent is a desert. The pinnacles in Western Australia is a unique desert. Once it had plenty of rains and was covered with forest. Water seeped below the surface where tree roots broke through the firm soil. Chemicals in the water mixed with sand formed hard columns of rock. Then the climate turned dryer and the forest died down. The whole area got turned into a desert. Winds eroded the surface soil and exposed tree trunk shaped hard rocks. There are several Aborigines who still live a primitive life. Kangaroo with a pouch under the belly is a unique mammal. The Great Barrier Reef extends to almost 2,000 km along its northeast coast. It is the largest structure made by living creature. It is also a colorful area in the world.

Antarctica: Ronald Edmundson, a Norwegian explorer, was the first to reach Antarctica on way to South Pole with sledge dogs which pulled supplies in 1911. This continent doesn't have any permanent population although it has a very vast area of 5100400 sq km. 90% of the land is covered with ice. This is the world largest desert with arid and barren land. The huge sheet of ice which covers the land is more than 4 km thick at places. The remaining 2% of land if rocky, uneven, and lifeless just like the surface of the moon. The seas around the continent are full of fish and plankton, drawing large numbers of whales, seals, and penguins to the coastal waters. The average annual snowfall is 12 cm which keeps the summer temperature at -57 C and winter temperature at -90 C. The ice sheet at the South Pole is 2,800 m thick. The highest mountain peak, Vinson Massif, is 5,140 m and Mount Erebus (3,846 m) is an active volcano. Mosses, lichens and one variety of grass are the largest plants. Research scientists living for short periods in specially built stations that protect them from intense cold are Antarctica's only inhabitants. Under a treaty, this continent cannot become the property of any one nation. Rather it is the property of all of humanity as it is the largest reservoir of fresh water. Only 11 countries have set up research centers on the continent.

CHAPTER TWO

Dinosaurs

The last five decades of the 20th century saw the maximum number of changes in the world. Frontiers of learning and knowledge in every field were broken. New inventions completely changed the world. It was during this period that the fossils and eggs of the supposedly the largest creatures on the earth were discovered in almost all parts of the world. They were named "dinosaurs." These discoveries generated considerable excitement about them. It started a systematic study about these prehistoric creatures. Experts all over the world compared their notes and came out with startling facts.

They developed from Saurischian Reptiles at the end of the Paleozoic Era (some 200 million years ago). The most ancient of them was Coelophysis. It was a good runner and very agile. The size of these animals from the Jurassic Period is calculated from their skeletons and footprints. The Diplodocus and Brontosaurus were more than 65 feet (20 meters) long. The largest of them was if 115 feet (35 meters) but very little is known about them. This animal would have been able to graze at the height of 6 story buildings and would have weighed more than 100 tons. Contrary to the popular belief, most of the dinosaurs were peaceful herbivores. The largest were Quadrupeds and spent most of their time grazing grass and trees. To save them from carnivores, they had developed different techniques such as hiding in water and running away. Some had bodies covered in hard scales, spikes, or horns which made them very difficult to kill. Among them was the Camptosaurus (1 foot long). Styracosaurus was another plant eater. It had horns and six long spikes around its neck and a sharp nose horn. Triceratops was the largest horned dinosaur. It had three horns- a forty-inch horn over each eye and a short on its nose. It was able to charge like a rhinoceros and could even beat a Tyrannosaur which was a carnivore, the biggest and fiercest of all the dinosaurs. Tyrannosaurus' were 46 feet long and stood as tall as a house. It used its huge jaws and six-inch teeth to eat other dinosaurs. A fight between a triceratops and a tyrannosaur must have been a violent sight.

The Chasmosaurus looked like the triceratops. Its enormous collar, packed with teeth, its deadly horns and a powerful mouth made it a fearful animal all though it was an herbivore. The Stegosaurus had hard scales, large flat plates all along the back, and four spikes on its tail. There was another group of dinosaurs, the Ankylosaurus, which also had the hard scales equivalent of armor. It allowed them to fend off attacks by large carnivorous dinosaurs. Some also had a ball of bones at the end of their tails and used it as a weapon. They were big and low on the grass which made them look even more massive.

The Ornithischian dinosaurs were Ornithopods, which had several bird-like features. Their feet had three claws at the front. Pteranodon was one of the largest flying reptiles. Its body was only the size of a turkey, but its great wings stretched out 23 feet from tip to tip. It glided over the sea and swooped down to catch fish. Some dinosaurs such as the Hadrosaurus had a snout that was flat like a duck. Inside this horned structure was a mouth with 2,000 pointed teeth set on several levels to act as a perfect tool for crushing vegetation and stripping trees. Their skull was extended by a crest that made their cries louder and a deterrent. Lambeosaurus was duck-billed dinosaur. It had a broad, flat jaw that looked like a duck's bill. Parasaurolophus had the longest crest of all- up to six feet. The crest was connected to its nostril and helped it smell enemies. Euoplocephalus was armored with lumps of spikes for protection. When in danger, it crouched down and tucked its legs under its body. It could also swing its heavy clubbed tail.

Most of the dinosaurs were big and heavy but some were very small, not bigger than a rooster and running like an ostrich, upright on its back feet. An example of a small dinosaur was the Compsognathus. It was about the size of a chicken. They hunted lizards and little woodland animals. It was a skillful and fast hunter.

All carnivorous dinosaurs were bipeds. Some were big; others small, some were hunters; other ate dead animal. "Why were dinosaurs so big?" is a question that cannot be answered easily. According to modern biology, the bigger an animal is the easier it is to keep warm. Perhaps, the great dinosaurs could survive the cool night due to their big bodies. To protect them against the cold birds, have feathers and have their hair. Reptiles only have their bare skin. The ratio of body surface to volume is much less for a larger animal than for a smaller one. Thus, large animals lose less heat and that the heat is lost more slowly.

Such big animals were also having one brain in their thick skulls just like other animals. This made them the creatures with low intelligence. The Stegosaurus of the Jurassic Period was a huge creature, but its brain was the size of a nut.

Dinosaurs did not live in the water but some like huge Apotosaurus, spent most of their time next to lakes or in marshes. There they were able to cool their bodies in water. There they used their long necks forage for food. Their feet were more like those of elephants rather than hippos.

Like the buffalo of today, the herbivorous dinosaurs sometimes formed herds to impress their enemies like tyrannosaurus. Twenty iguanodons, preserved in mud, were found in Belgium. This shows that the sauropods lived in herds just like the Godrosaurus.

The age of the dinosaurs (Mesozoic Era) lasted 160 million years. It was a time of great change: the continents separated, the climate changed, the plants and animals evolved. Between the appearance of Pangaea, a super continent, from the ocean in the Triassic Period and the Jurassic Period, the southern area Gondwanaland detached itself from the north, Laurasia. In the coming years, Gondwanaland was further divided into many parts making Africa, South America, and Australia. New climates were created by new mountain ranges. These changes account for the distribution of the species throughout the world. That is why the fossils of dinosaurs throughout the world.

All dinosaurs laid eggs. These eggs in the shape of fossils have also been found in most parts of the world. The excavation of eggs from a little mound of about six feet square in Mongolia has helped us to get a better idea how these creatures grew up. The newborn was defenseless, and their parents had to protect them from predatory dinosaurs such as the Oviraptor, which was a great egg-eater. After hatching, all big dinosaurs underwent a period of tremendous growth. Likes of Apatosaurus on reaching adulthood had increased their weight 3,000 times. A whale, in contrast, increases its weight only 50 times.

End of Era: It is not yet exactly known why a great many species like these creatures suddenly disappeared 65 million years ago. Perhaps at the end of Cretaceous Period, most of the large reptiles and dinosaurs became extinct. The reason of this disappearance is a mystery. Paleontologists have a few theories. Maybe a huge meteorite struck earth and changed the climate, or there was a devastating volcanic eruption, or the sea levels fell. What might have happened is a guessing game. But this disaster marked the end of the Mesozoic Era and the beginning of the Tertiary Period.

CHAPTER THREE

Animal Kingdom

Life on the earth has existed for millions of years in different forms with some 10 million known species. They are divided into: Vertebrates (animals with backbones) and Invertebrates (animals without backbones).

Invertebrates

a. Crustaceans: They include crabs, lobsters, and barnacles. There are 40,000 different species of these animals and most of them are found in the sea. They have joined legs and generally breathe with gills.
b. Annelids: They are in the form of worms and have 8,700 species.
c. Mollusks: animals like snails with a hard-external shell, live in the ocean. Their species number is 100,000.
d. Insects: The known species of insects are 800,000. But according to rough estimates, 30 million of them may exist. They include butterflies, grasshoppers, and ants. Most of them live on land.
e. Lower invertebrates: They are the simple animals. All of them are headless creatures like jellyfish, coral, sponge, phyla and may have several million species.

Vertebrates

a. Amphibians: There 4300 different species of amphibians. They live on land but breed in water. They include frogs, salamanders. They involved from fishes more than 350 million years ago. They are cold-blooded animals. \
b. Reptiles: They involved from amphibians some 300 million years ago. Out of 6,100 species, crocodiles, lizards, snakes, and turtles are the most prominent. They are also cold-blooded animals.
c. Mammals: They are the animals which suckle their young ones. They evolved from Reptiles about 200 million years ago. They have only 4500 species but are the most successful in the Animal Kingdom. All of them are warm-blooded creatures, meaning, they maintain a constant temperature in all seasons. Men, lion, ape, and goats are covered in this group.
d. Fishes: They evolved from invertebrates some 540 million years ago. They live in water and are cold-blooded. There are some 22,000 species alive today which include: salmon, sharks, electric eel, and goldfish.
e. Birds: Some 140 million years ago, they evolved from reptiles. They have 9,000 species and can fly with use of wings. All of them lay eggs and are warm-blooded like mammals.

Mammals:

Elephants- Royalty among Animals: It is the heaviest mammal on land. A matured elephant may weigh up to 6800 kg and extend more than 3 meters. The gestation period is 22 months. Only one calf is born per pregnancy. At the time of birth, the calf weighs 60-135 kg. The life span is about 70 years. They are found mostly in equatorial Africa and Southeast Asia. East African elephants are the biggest of all. Their ancestor, Woolly Mammoth, roamed freely in the arctic regions of Europe, Asia, and western North America some 40,000 years ago. They had long hair and bigger, curved tusks. They became extinct about 8,000 years ago. American zoologists have dug out the whole body of a mammoth from the Polar Regions recently. It is in good shape and may figure in the National History Museum (New York). Elephants' trunks have 40,000 muscles and tendons. They make it highly flexible and incredibly strong. Elephants love water and are great swimmers. They are known to swim 48 km at a time. In olden days, they were used in wars just like the tanks of today. It was a symbol of prestige and royalty. Even today it shas not outlived its utility. It is vegetarian animal and survives on leaves, sugar canes etc.

Zebras- The Striped Brothers of the Horse: It is a timid, wild animal found only in Africa. The stripes on their body differentiate from a horse or a donkey. They are as unique as our fingerprints are. It means two zebras are the same. A matured zebra may be 120-160 cm tall and weigh 300-450 kg. They are vegetarians that survive on grass and live in herds of 10-12. The gestation period is 11-13 months and they can live for 20 years. Only one young one is born per pregnancy. At the time of the annual migration, thousands of zebras can be seen moving towards the north in game reserves like the Serengeti, East Africa.

Rhinoceroses- The Bad-Tempered Devils: It is one of the most feared and bad-tempered wild animals. They are 5-6.5 feet in height and can weigh up to 3600 kg. Like other animals, it also has horns but only rhino sports them on its nose. It is used to save the young ones from predators. Gestation period is 15-16 months and only one calf is born per pregnancy. It may live from 40-45 years. Generally, the mother and the young one stay together otherwise it is a solitary creature. African Rhinos have 2 horns while its Asian cousin has 1 horn. It is also a vegetarian animal and survives on grass and the branches of trees. Apart from the forests of Africa, it is found in the dense of Eastern Asia including Assam, Sunderbun (India), Sumatra, Java, and Borneo (Indonesia). The Sumatran Rhino has much hair on its body and is the smallest of all the rhinos with 2 horns. They can run at the speed of 45 kmph.

Hippopotamuses- The Kings of the River: This round and rotund animal resembles the rhino. One mature hippo can attain the height of up to 5.4 feet and weigh 400 kg. Its gestation period is 7-8 months. Generally, one or at the most two calves are born per pregnancy. They can live up to 54 years. Grass is their stable food. They are found in lakes and the rivers of the Sub-Saharan Africa in groups that may include 150 animals. They spend so much time in the water that the ancient Greeks nicknamed them as, "the Riverhorse." This name is popular in Asia even today. After spending 18 hours in the water, it comes out at night to graze. While grazing they move miles away from the water but return to their habitat by daybreak. They sit, almost submerged, and still see and breathe for quite a long time. The babies can even swim before they can walk.

Camels- The Ships of the Desert: Camels are the part of life of people who live in the deserts of Asia, Africa, and the Middle East. It is one of the tallest animals on land which can carry loads equal to their own weight and tolerate the extreme heat and cool of the desert climate. People drink camel's milk, eat its meat, use the dung for fuel, and weave the hair into cloth. Its shoulder height reaches 6-7.5 feet and it may weight 300-690 kg on maturity. It survives on leaves, herbs, and grass. The gestation period is 12-14 months. Only one young one is born per pregnancy. It can live for 30-40 years. Camels have long eyelashes to keep sand out of their eyes. Besides a top and bottom eyelid, a third lid helps remove sand. They can shut their nostrils to prevent sand from blowing in. The nostrils drain into their mouth. So, they can use their own mucus for moisture. There are two types of camels- the domesticated drome dary (has one hump) and the wild Bactrian (has two humps and hair). The name, "camel," comes from the ancient Arabic word," gamel," which means, "carrying a burden."

Llamas- A Dwarf Camel: Llamas are the relatives of camels. They are not as tall as their elderly relatives and do not have humps. A grown-up llama can have a shoulder height of 2.3-4.3 feet and weigh 35-155 kg. They also live off grass and leaves. The gestation period is 11-12 months and only one offspring is born per pregnancy. It can live for 15-24 years. Unlike camels, they live in mountains. Their blood is specially adapted for reduced oxygen and freezing temperatures at high altitudes. They are used in the rugged Andes Mountains in the same way as the camels in the deserts. They are so strong that they can carry more weight than their body. They were the main stay of the Inca Empire in Peru, South America. The Incas held them sacred. They fashioned their images out of silver to represent the white llama- a symbol of royalty.

Giraffes-The Tallest Creatures on Land: This tallest wild animal usually grows to about 5.8 meters in height with a weight of 1800 kg. One calf is born per pregnancy. In the wild a giraffe generally lives for about 26 years but in captivity, it survives up to 36 years. It is an herbivorous animal and lives off leaves and fresh shoots. It is an African animal which is found in central, eastern, and southern African forests. The giraffes take a stride of about 4.5 meters. They are timid and prefer to avoid trouble and can spot danger kilometers away because of their height and keen eyesight. Like camels, it can go for weeks without water. When it drinks water, it bends its front legs and then brings its neck to the water level. Its tongue is about 2 feet long and helps in stripping leafy branches clean. When the first giraffe was brought to Paris in 1827, the Parisians went wild for "giraffe style." Men started to wear coats patterned after giraffe's spots and women had their hair done up in a style resembling the giraffe's head.

Buffalos- The Wrestlers among Animals: Bison is the European name for buffalo. At the time of the first settlement of whites in North America at the end of the 15th century, some 50 million bison were roaming on the land. By the end of the 19th century, they were nearly wiped out by the European settlers. It was a wild animal with thick manes and a muscular hump. The shoulder height of a mature buffalo varies from 5-6.5 feet and weighs from 350-1000 kg. Its gestation period is 9.5 months. Normally, one calf is born per pregnancy. It usually lives 18-22 years on prairie herbs and grass in the summer but on mosses and lichens in the winter. In America, Europe, and Africa, it is still a wild animal but in Asia it has been tamed centuries ago and today, it is a main source of milk. It is also used to draw cart, carry load, and plough the field.

Its cousin, the yak of Asia, lives at higher altitudes than most mammals. Although a few still live in the wild, the yaks have also been domesticated and are used by people of the Himalayas as a beast of burden and for its meat, milk, and wool.

Deer Family

Antelopes and Gazelles: They are found in Africa and Asia and are usually noticed for their horns which come in unusual shapes. They can weigh up to 70 kg and reach the shoulder height of 3.45 feet in maturity. Surviving on herbs, grass, leafy shrubs, cacti, and other plants, they can live for 12 years. After a gestation period of 8.5 months, the female delivers 1 or 2 calves. It can run at 18 kmph. One type of antelope grows antlers (12 horns) which fall off each year. But this happens in the case of only males, of course, in caribou of Arctic regions, both male and female grow antlers. They live in large herds and move along in a steady stream. No land mammal travels as far in a single year as the caribou. The European caribou are called reindeer and they live near the North Pole. They have red noses from the cold and can live in below 0-degree temperature. The reindeers are the proverbial sleigh driver of Santa Clause.

The deer family has some 45 species. They are distributed worldwide. Their habitat varies from forests to desert to the arctic tundra. Antlers are the specialty with them. A big rack of antlers is fierce looking. The antlers' primary purpose, however, is a social one. Males (called bucks) with big antlers are more attractive to females (called does). They are a sign of good health and those would rather mate with healthy bucks. Once the mating season (January-April) the antlers simply fall off. They normally fall off one at a time. The huge palmate antlers, meaning, "Shaped like the palm of hands," of a moose can weigh 36 kg. In the summer, the antlers provide a cooling system. They carry a supply of blood which is cooled by the outside air before it re-circulates through the body. When the antlers fall off, the blood shuts off.

Its cousin, the wild beast, in Africa lives in big herds and is not as quick as the other species are. That is why all carnivores hunt them. They are easy prey even for crocodiles and hyenas. They also take part in the annual migration along with zebras.

Moose, elk, and eland, of East Africa, are among the biggest deer species while pudu, of South America, is the smallest one.

Carnivore:

Any animal that eats meat is defined as a carnivore. All carnivores have sharp teeth, sharp claws, and a strong stomach to raw meat. They also have sharp ears, a good nose, and keen eyesight to outrun, outsmart, and overpower their prey. For this reason, they are also called predators.

Lions- Kings of the Forest: They are the most social members of the cat family. A group or pride is led by one to three adult males. The other members of the pride are several females and their cubs. Females are responsible for hunting prey and raising their cubs whereas the males protect the territory of the pride which may be around 400 square km. The head and body length varies from 4.6 feet to 8.2 feet. Males are slightly bigger than females. The weight at maturity reaches up to 250 kg. The gestation period is 3-4 months and usually 3-4 young ones are born per pregnancy. Their life span varies from 13-30 years. A male lion consumes as much as 30 kg of meat in a single meal. They often lounge around for 20 hours a day to digest their food. The lioness moves the cubs to safety by grabbing the scruff of their necks without hurting them. They run faster than males, which have thick manes on their necks. Hyenas are their natural enemies because both compete for the same sources of food, especially on the African savannah, the best habitat of the lions. The lions are one of the biggest members of the cat family but cannot climb up on trees. However, the lions of Lake Manyara game park, Tanzania have developed this skill also; perhaps the presence of tsetse fly on land has forced them to do so.

Tigers- The Lone Hunters: Tigers are the biggest and most ferocious cats. Unlike lions, they prefer to live along except when a female is tending her cubs. Its head and body length ranged from 4.5- 9.2 feet and they weight about 65-380 kg at maturity. The gestation period is only 3 months and usually 2-3 cubs are born per pregnancy. It can live up to 25 years. Its habitats range from the snowy forests of Siberia to the muggy jungles of Southeast Asia. These places allow the animal to hide as it stalks its prey which includes large mammals like pigs, deer, wild oxen, and buffalo. It is a nocturnal animal as it hunts mostly at night. They can see in dim light, many times better than a human, because their eyes have a dense layer of cells in their retinas that are sensitive to low light. These cells also reflect any light that shines on them, making the tiger's eyes appear to burn. The Siberian tiger is the world's largest cat. It measures up to 9.2 feet from head to tail and weighs up to 380 kg. White tigers are a rare breed and some 30 years ago, six white tigers were found in the forest of Rewa in M.P. (in India). It was a pleasant surprise because this breed was thought to be extinct. Today, about 100 white tigers live in the zoos of the world. The population of the tigers is dwindling throughout the world. They are being hunted thoughtlessly for their skin and bones which are used in China for making energy-giving medicines. Several "Save the Tiger" programs are on in India and Southeast Asia. It is hoped that these programs will be successful in creating a breathing space for the tigers.

Leopards- The Shrewd and Cunning Hunters: Leopards live in Africa and Asia. Its body is sleek and graceful with a long tail. Its light body enables it to climb up the trees easily. The length of a matured leopard is 3-6 feet long. It acquires 28-90 kg in weight. A pregnant female delivers 2-3 young ones after a gestation period of 3-3.5 months. Generally, they live for 15-23 years. Its spots take the form of ring-shaped patterns called rosettes. It can drag its prey's body up a tree and stores the food this weigh to keep it save from other animals. It will feed on the kill for several days. The Snow Leopard lives in the high mountains of the Himalayas. It is a champion jumper and can leap up to 15 meters in a single bound. In the summer, it climbs the bare rocks as high as 6,000 meters but in the winter, it prowls the forest below 1,800 meters.

Another variety is the Black Panther. It looks black from a distance; however, its spots are visible on its coat on a closer look. A single liter of ten includes both black and spotted leopard cubs.

Jaguars-The Greatest Hunters of South America: Jaguar looks and acts somewhat like a leopard. Its home is Central and South America. In comparison to leopards, its body is thicker and mature jaguars can way up to 158 kg and leave 3-6 feet in length. After a gestation period of 3-3.5 months, a female delivers a liter of 2-4. Its longevity is up to 22 years. In the equatorial rainforest, they stalk all creatures, great or small. After a hunt, a jaguar drags the prey to a secluded place before eating it. In addition to being a good hunter, it is an excellent swimmer. It prefers to live near fresh water, where it can catch fish, turtles, and small alligators. Ancient Peruvians revered the jaguar as the God of the Night. They believed that the spots on its coat stood for stars in the sky.

Cheetahs- The Fastest Runners: Cheetahs live in Africa and part of the Middle East. It cannot measure up to the big cats like lions, tigers, and jaguars, but prefers to hunt by day. It is the quickest among all the cats and does not stalk its prey. Rather, it pursues the prey at a speed of 110 kmph and wears it down in the open. Reaching about 70 kg, the cheetah outweighs other small cats. The body length reached up to 5 feet. The gestation period is 3 months and 3-6 offspring are born per pregnancy. It can live up to 19 years and it is a poor climber. Cubs live with their mother for 18 months. After that, they leave in a pack of 2-4. It is a fast animal because of its flexible backbone which expands and contracts like a coiled spring. In ancient India, the noblemen tamed and trained cheetahs to hunt. Such a cheetah would run after game, knock it down, then wait nearby for the master. The pharaohs of Egypt also used cheetahs for this purpose.

Small Cats: Except Australia and Antarctica, all parts of the world have small but ferocious cats. They vary from the smallest black footed (1-2 feet) to the largest Cougar of America (3-6 feet). The weight on maturity also varies in the same fashions from 2.8 kg to 103 kg. Their habitats also vary but, the majority lives in the forest or the dry, open country. Their gestation period is between 2-3 months and the liter at birth consists of 1-8 kittens. It may live for 15 years. None of these cats can roar because the bones in their voice box are joined too tightly to make a roaring sound. The bobcat, the most common wild cat in North America, has a short tail. It lives in swamps, grasslands, and deserts and prey on fish and amphibians. Most cats avoid water, but the fishing cat jumps in the water and catches fish. Among lynx, the male helps care for his young. He brings foot for the mother and the newborn until the kittens are 5 months old. The Cougar, or Puma, is a superb jumper and leap up to 18 feet in one bound up into a tree. The mink cat of Siberia has been widely hunted for its valuable coat. It is also on the verge of extinction.

Bears-The Big Brothers:

Bears, especially the brown grizzly, are the largest carnivore on land. It can weigh up to 700 kg and stand up to 2.8 meters tall. Despite having canine teeth of a carnivore, a bear eats more plants than meat. Thus, it is an omnivore. Honey is a delicious dish for a bear living in the equatorial forest but the colder regions of North America, munching on grass, berries, roots, and bulbs and occasional salmon, elk, or moose, the grizzly stores up enough body fat to be able to sleep through the entire winter. After a gestation period of 6-9 months, 1-4 cubs are born. Bears can live up to 30 years. They spend most of the winter dozing in a den but wakes up quickly if disturbed. During this time, the pregnant female gives birth, and then nurses the cubs in her sleep. Grizzly bears walk in each other's paw prints. That is why their tracks are so deep in the Denali Park. Some bear trails cut 15-centimeter-deep into the solid ground. Black Bears are good climbers.

Polar bears are hunters on ice. In the absence of plants, the huge mammal must be a crafty hunter to survive. They prey on fish, sea birds, and ringed seals. A full-grown polar bear may tower 3.5 meters tall and some have reached more than 800 kg. An excellent swimmer, the polar bear can swim across 65 km of open water. A layer of 7.5-centimeter-thick fat keeps it warm in almost freezing water.

Pandas living in the mountains of Central China are the near relatives of bears. Their head and body length are 4-5 feet and weigh 75-160 kg. It survives on bamboo shoots and roots. Their strong jaws and flat molars chew 35 kg or bamboo a day. Pandas are born blind and with skimpy, white fur. Their birth weight might be as low as 90 grams-less than that of a mouse. It means their parents outweigh them 1,400:1. No others placental mammal has a higher weight ratio of adult to young one.

Wolves- The Dog Family on the Prowl:

Wolfs are the largest members of the dog family. They are found in all Northern Hemisphere habitats except tropical forests and live in family groups with an adult pair and their young ones. The gestation period is only 2 months. In the wild, they usually live for 4 years. When the pups are born, the mother tends them in her den and the father brings food. The body length of an adult wolf is 3.2 feet-5.2 feet and it weighs 20-80 kg. They are co-operative hunters. Three wolves work together to isolate one animal from the herd, and then drive it towards the other wolves waiting in the ambush. Their howl is the way they communicate with each other. Like all carnivores, wolves have sharp, interlocking side teeth called canines, use them as deadly weapons to grip prey and pierce flesh. An arctic wolf leaps from one ice floe to another as it searches its territory for food. They hunt caribou, musk oxen, and arctic hares. A single wolf pack may roam a territory of 2,600 km.

The devil coyote is a near relative of the wolf, which rules the desert. It has a black coat and a white mane. It is faster than all other wolves. When it is thirsty, it makes a small hole in a cactus and drinks its juice. It holds the liquid in its throat for a week. Its coat is bushy which does not allow the heat to penetrate its skin. They survive by hunting rabbits, mice, toads, and snakes.

Bats- Lords of Darkness:

Bats are the only mammals that fly. A bat's wing is a hand whose stretched out fingers are joined by leathery skin. They fly with a sculling motion just like a swimmer. Flying as high as 3,000 meters, they can reach the speed of 100 km per hour. There are 986 species of bats. They live almost everywhere except Antarctica and the Arctic. Most of them survive on insects. A mature bat can weigh up to 1.5 kg. Their gestation period is 1.5-4.8 months. Only one offspring is born per pregnancy. They can live up to 15-20 years. They roost hanging upside down in large colonies. Some caves hold millions of them. When winter comes, the bats go into a deep sleep in their roost. They die if disturbed.

Vampire bats are blood-thirsty creatures. They are found only in Central and South America. They prefer the blood of cows, pigs, and chickens. Their bite is so painless that it doesn't even wake those animals.

Great Apes

Orangutans (Van Manus): Orangutans are the most mysterious of all the great apes. They live in swampy forests of Borneo, Sumatra, and Malaysia. They prefer to live in trees and love to eat. The head and body length of this primate at maturity is 4-5 feet and weigh 30-90 kg. After the gestation period of about 9 months, females give birth to one child. It can live up to 59 years. They have small families as a female will only have one baby after 8 or 9 years. When night approaches, orangutans build white platform nests made from branches high up in the trees. There they sleep free from predators. They are highly shy but learn human activities if taught. In Singapore, the author saw an orangutan dining at the table just like a human being.

Gorillas- The Giants of the Jungle: Gorillas are the natives of the forests of Central Africa. They live in small groups called troops and wander in the search of leaves, vine, and bamboo shoots to eat for half a day. They laze in the sun and play with their children. If another gorilla threatens, the adult male roars up and beats his chest to frighten the intruder just like and Indian wrestler. Gorillas are the largest of the great apes. A matured ape can weigh up to 275 kg and stands as tall as 6 feet. There strong arms can span nearly 3 meters. Their gestation period is almost 9 months and on baby is born per pregnancy. The life span is 50-55 years. They are gentle and peace-loving and sleep in nests that are built on the ground. It is a flat platform made of leaves, branches, and moss. In many ways they are like humans. Their palms are quite like us. Gorilla's babies cling to their mothers until they are 3 years old.

Chimpanzees are very similar to gorillas except that they are smarter. They have a longer life span of 60 years. Due to their friendly nature and ability to learn, they are called "party animals."

Kangaroos-The Bouncing Marsupial:

When they are born, they are tiny, naked, deaf, and blind. Still in the next 4 minutes they drag themselves over their mother's belly to a pouch of skin. Once inside, they are safe. They spend months of growing, resting, and eating in the mother's pouch all the time. At maturity, they acquire a length up to 5.2 feet and weigh 90 kg. They live in organized groups of 2-10 and can live for 20 years. Kangaroos are found only in Australia and New Guinea. They are great leapers. At that time, their enormous, powerful hind legs fling them along in huge bounds up to 48 km an hour. They jump an average of 9 meters per bound. Male kangaroos, called boomers, sometimes have fights that combine wrestling, boxing, kicking and just standing around. They will punch with their forelegs and kick with their powerful hind legs. They survive on grass. In the absence of predators, the control of their population becomes a problem for the Australian government.

Whales-The Largest Mammals:

Whales, the largest mammals, live in the vast world of oceans. They are warm-blooded, breathe air through lungs, have hair on their bodies and nurse their babies just like other mammals on land. They have evolved flippers, fins, and flukes to equip them for the deep-sea life. They have 10 species. At maturity, their length and weight vary from 5.5-31 meters (10-102 feet) and 2,850-160,000 kg (equal to 22 elephants) respectively. After the gestation period of 10-13 months, only one calf is bor. They can live up to 114 years and survive on small squid, fish, and planktons. Except for the Sperm Whale, all the largest whales are toothless (i.e. baleen). The Blue Whale is the largest of all. They exchange air through blowholes that are on top of their head. Humpback Whales catch fish with a 'bubble net.' They surround the fish and blow bubbles, frightening the fish into the middle of the nest, where they are easy prey. Dolphins, Killer Whales, and Porpoises have teeth in their jaws. They are fastest sea mammals speeding through the ocean at 45 km per hour. Sperm Whales can dive deeper and stay under the water longer than any other mammal (up to 40 minutes). Killer Whales are the only crustaceans that eat other mammals. Dolphins are the friendliest whales for man. They comprise of more than 40 species. They follow complicated instructions and are as intelligent as chimpanzee. They move swiftly, swimming in tight formations. They may be 3.6-13 feet long, weigh 25-250 kg and live for 6-40 years.

Seals and Walruses:

Seals and Walruses can stay on land for a long period. They come ashore to sleep, mate, and bear their young. Seals can use their flippers as feet when they are on land. Sea lions and fur seals have ears, but walruses have no ears. They are powerful swimmers and deep divers. Their body length varies from 3.6 feet to 19.7 feet as their weight varies from 27.3 to 700 kg. After the gestation period of 9-12 months, one or two babies are born. They can live up to 30 years. Seals and walruses are found in Arctic, temperate, and sub-tropical waters along the seacoast, rocky islands, sandy beaches, and ice floes. They survive on krill, squid, and fish. A thick lining of fat under the skin called blubber protects them in their polar environment. Earless seals like sea lions can turn their hind flippers forward to function like feet on land and ice. Walruses can move better on land than earless seals which slither along like giant worms. Elephant seal, the largest of all, has a trunk like nose which help it shout out a deafening roar to be heard for nearly a kilometer.

Second in size, the walruses have a bristly mustache used for finding shellfish. They're ivory tusks can grow up to 1 meter long, used in fighting and climbing on ice. They live near the moving pack ice of the Arctic Ocean.

Manatees-Mild Mannered Mammal of the Sea:

Manatees are the most threatened species of sea mammals. They are large and lumbering creatures with whiskered snouts, front flippers, and pedal shaped tails. Once they were thought to be mermaids of mythology. They are the only vegetarian sea mammals. They can grow up to 14 feet long and weigh 600 kg. Only one young are born after the gestation period of 12-13 months. They can live up to 30 years. They nurse their young through a teat behind their flippers for 2 years. They are found in coastal waters and the rivers of North, Central South America, and Western Africa and survive on aquatic plants. Their steady feeding on sea grasses help keep coastal water ways unclogged. For ages, the sailors thought that manatees with their fish-like tails and human faces were the mythical mermaids. Even Christopher Columbus, after spotting the manatees in the Caribbean, claimed to have seen three mermaids, though he added that, "They are not as beautiful as they are painted."

CHAPTER FOUR

Wonders Of The World: Ancient

In the first century BC, Antipater, a Greek writer of Sidon, prepared a list of the most spectacular buildings of his time. After some time, they became known as The Seven Wonders of the Word. Why he prepared this list is not known; perhaps he intended to make the first tourist pamphlet for the people living in the Eastern Mediterranean region. The number was fixed to seven; it was considered sacred, and often associated with religion for some mysterious reasons.

All these wonders were situated in the south, east and north. It is noteworthy that people in the west considered the Mediterranean Sea as the hub of civilization. They had very little knowledge about the east and its civilizations, in the absence of information, communication and technology. Therefore, they considered the structures known to them at the time as the original wonders. If we evaluate the original seven from present day standards, it would be unfair and unjust towards those master artists of the east.

Over the past centuries, most of the original wonders collapsed and fell to ruin. If we remember that there is something amazing about them- their colossal size, the remarkable way they were built, the typical material used, and their beautify- we would surlily appreciate them. What they all have in common though is their unfailing ability to make people marvel at their very existence.

The original seven wonders were: Pyramid of Giza, Hanging Garden of Babylon, Statue of Zeus, The Temple of Artemis, The Tomb of Mausolus, the Colossus of Rhodes and Pharos lighthouse.

Pyramids of Egypt:

The Great Pyramids of Egypt are the world's oldest buildings: they truly are the wonders of the world. They are gigantic stone tombs of the rulers of ancient Egypt. The most famous Egyptian pyramids are the three that stand near Giza. They are five miles west of Cairo, situated on the borders of the Libyan Desert. They have a square base and the four sides are shaped like triangle, which meet at the top.

The largest of them was built by Pharaoh Khufu, or Cheops, who lived about 2,600 BC. Its base covers 13 acres. The top point stands about 451 feet above the ground. The original height was 481 feet. It is estimated that this pyramid contains 2300000 stone blocks. The average weight of each block is about 2.5 tons. The size is about 40 cubic feet. Ages ago, the pyramid was covered with polished stone, all carefully fitted together. These have long since disappeared. Only the rough blocks remain.

Deep inside the pyramid are the tomb chambers. They are reached by narrow corridors. The entrance to the pyramid is on the north side, about 48 feet above the ground. This corridor descends gradually to a level passage, which opens into a room below the Earth. From the first corridor lies another, which leads to the chamber of queens and the Great Halls. This hall is a high, narrow vault which ends in a passage leading to the king's chamber. Polished granite lines the wall of this room, which contains the stone coffin of the king. This pyramid took 30 years to complete and nearly 20,000 laborers worked on it.

Near the Great Pyramid stand the second and third pyramid of Khafre (Chepheon) and Mycernius. A few yards away stands the statue of the Sphinx. The statue of the great sphinx was built some 5,000 years ago. It sits as a garden deity to the pyramids of Giza. An impressive 60 feet (20 m) high and 240 feet (73 m long), the sphinx has a human face and a body of a lion. Nobody knows whose face it resembles.

Hanging Gardens of Babylon:

The Hanging Gardens of Babylon bloom as a living green miracle in a desert city. This was a group of five gardens, built in the form of a square. They were constructed about 600 BC and rose in a series of terraces to a height of about 350 feet. Each garden contained trees, shrubs, and flowers of various kinds. It is believed that Emperor Nebuchadnezzar ordered the gardens built to honor his wife Amytis, who missed the green and hilly landscape of her homeland to the north: Persia. The lush garden provided a cool refuge from the burning heat of the desert in which Babylon (modern Iraq) stood. In 539 BC, the Persians conquered Babylon and its independence was lost forever. No glamour was left. As the years went by, people left the city. By 200 AD, it was deserted and in ruins. Nobody knows exactly when the hanging garden lost their façade, or even where they were. Archaeologists now claim that they have discovered the forts which formed the base for the gardens near the palace.

A roman writer visited the garden long after the fall of Babylon and found they still standing. He described them as a series of vaulted terraces, built pyramid like (one on the top of another) and flanked by walls more than 20 feet thick. Each terrace contained soil deep enough for trees to grow. Exotic plants and flowers were cascaded over the trees. Cyprus palms and trees provided shade. The air was heavy with the scent of aromatic plants and flowers. To irrigate the gardens, water was pumped from the nearby Euphrates River through a hidden network of pipes leading to the terraces. Since the third century, they have become a façade of history.

The Statue of Zeus:

This giant and magnificent statue was made by the master Greek sculptor Phidias in 433 BC as his tribute to the king of Greek gods at Olympia. The statue took up the whole width of the temple Aisle. According to a contemporary writer, it was 40 feet tall. If it was able to stand up (Zeus was sitting on the throne with Nike, the goddess of victory, in the palm of his right hand a shining scepter on which an eagle was perched, symbolizing his power) his head would have gone through the roof. This statue was carved out of ivory. His hair and beard were made of gold, and his eyes were set with precious gemstones. It sat on a magnificent cedar wood throne, inlayed with ivory, gold, ebony and other precious stones.

The statue soon came to be considered among the wonders of the world. For ancient Greeks, it was the symbol of perfection. Every year, thousands of people paid their homage to Zeus at the shrine of Olympia. It is said that roman Emperor Caligula wanted to take the statue to Rome, where he would replace its head with that of his own. When his soldiers came to take it, the statue laughed wildly. The terrified soldiers ran away. The statue remained in the temple for centuries. The shrine lay neglected in roman times. Finally, in 394 AD it was taken to Constantinople, capital of the Byzantine Empire, to have been destroyed by fire in 475 AD.

Temple of Artemis: Diana:

A building used for worship is called a temple. They have been built since earliest times, in many parts of the world. Most temples are built to honor a god or a goddess. In the same way, the temple of Artemis was built to honor its namesake (Diana) at Ephesus in modern Turkey. This temple was destroyed in 262 AD. Some remains compel us to think of its greatness. It covered nearly two acres. About 100 graceful 60 ft columns held up its gently sloping roof. Around 550 BC, king Croesus of Lydia built this magnificent temple following his conquest of the Greek city of Ephesus. Inside the temple was an inner room, called the sanctuary that housed the splendid statue of the goddess. It was decorated with precious stones and metals. Popularly known as Artemision, the temple became famous and attracted worshippers from far and wide. The temple was the largest in the area during its time.

Rectangular, it was 170 ft wide and 366 ft long. The temple had columns which ran parallel to its wall. The columns at the front were decorated with intricate sculptures of the famous feats of god and heroes. It became famous not only for its size, but also for its sculptures.

One night in 356 BC, a mad man named Herostrautus set fire to the temple. The roof caved in, the columns collapsed, and the statue of the goddess crashed to the ground. When Alexander the Great conquered Ephesus, he offered to pay for the temple to be rebuilt. By 250 BC, the temple had been restored to its pristine glory and was soon acclaimed as one of the Seven Wonders of the World. Alexander never saw his dream fulfilled, as the temple took 150 years to rebuild.

According to Greek mythology, Artemis was a huntress and the goddess of fertility. The statue of Artemis was made of gold, silver, ebony and black stone. Time again took its toll. Storms and earthquakes destroyed the temple. Ruins sank into the ground, and the temple vanished from view. For centuries, no one knew where the temple stood. It was not until 1869 that and English engineer, J.T. Wood, discovered the exact location of the temple.

Tomb of Mausolus:

Tomb is any chamber in which the dead are buried. Some tombs are cut out of cork, and others are built out of ground. Ancient people used to use tombs to keep safe the body of the dead. Pyramids of Egypt are the old tomb of the world. Most Greek tombs were simple, but those of colonies of Asia Minor were very elaborate.

The most famous of them was the Tomb of Mausolus, at Halicarnassus in Caria, in modern Turkey. The world Mausoleum comes from the name of this tomb. It was one of the seven wonders of the ancient world. This was a magnificent burial place, built by Artemisia in 353 BC in the memory of her husband. Halicarna-roofus was on the southwest coast of Asia Minor. In 1800's, British scientists found valuable pieces of architecture and sculpture at the site. King Mausolus ruled over Caria in fourth century BC. He was an ambitious PC and attacked many neighboring cities and states. With the money from his conquests, he built a new capital. Towards the end of his life, he built himself a tomb which was a monument of his power. He wanted it to be the most magnificent tomb ever seen. After his death in 353 BC, his queen Artemisia fulfilled his dream. No expense was spared, and the finished tomb was so grand that it was called Mausoleum after Mausolus.

The base of this tomb covered an area measuring 156 ft by 105 ft. The finished tomb was 140 ft tall. It was designed to be a temple and tomb. It was built of gleaming white marble and consisted of three tiers on the top of which stood a temple and at the summit stood an enormous statue of Mausolus and Artemisia standing proudly in a horse drawn chariot. According to ancient manuscripts, Pythias, a great architect supervised the construction and Scopas, a Greek sculpture, oversaw the decoration. The Mausoleum was built in four stages, using the work force of many men.

Work continued the side of 10 years. The bottom part was built on a large platform. Inside this part lay a large burial chamber, containing the sarcophagus, or coffin, of king Mausoleus. Carved around the outside of the second section was the row of lions that guarded the tomb. Adoring the walls were sculpted decorations showing fierce battle between the Greeks and the legendary female warriors, the Amazons. The third level was built in a style of a Greek temple, with columns, it could only be reached by an internal staircase. The top level, supported by the columns, was a pyramid like-roof. It was crowned by a statue of Mausolus and Artemisia standing in a horse drawn chariot. The Mausoleum survived for centuries, but eventually fell into ruins. In the middle ages, crusaders knights took stoned from the ruins and used them to build a fortress. Fragments of the statue, including a huge chariot, measuring seven ft across are now on display at the British Museum.

The Colossus at Rhodes:

In ancient mythology, the island of Rhodes, off the coast of Turkey, was the island of Helios (the sun god). After successfully defending their island against invasion in 304 BC, the people of Rhodes built an enormous statue of Helios at the entrance of the harbor of the city of Rhodes, to thank their god for protecting them. The statue was called the colossus, because of its size. It towered to the height of 120 ft. and could be seen from far out to the sea. It was made of gleaming bronze. The crown of the sun raised around Helios's head, symbolizing his rule as sun god.

Tragically, only about 65 years after it was completed a violent earthquake brought the colossus tumbling down to the sea. No one knows exactly where the statue stood, or what it looked like. Some people believed it stood astride the entrance to the harbor, so that ships could sail between its legs. It is more likely, however that the statue was built in the city overlooking the harbor.

It was built by Charles, a pupil of famous Greek sculptor Lysippus. 12.5 tons of bronze and 7.5 tons of iron was used for it. The statue took 12 years to build and was eventually finished in 290 BC. The frame of the statue was made of iron and then covered with sheets of bronze. Inside the iron framework were huge blocks of stone. These were to give the colossus weight, this by making it stable so that it would not fall. Sadly, it was not strong enough and collapsed in 220 AD, after an earthquake. The ruins remained untouched for centuries. In 653 AD, Islamic armies invaded Rhodes and stole the bronze, taking it back to Syria. There, a merchant was said to have bought the bronze shell; he carried it away on 900 camels across the desert, to be melted down.

Paroslighthouse

This lighthouse was said to be built on an island in the bay of Alexandria, by Ptolemy 2 (309-246 BC). It was nearly 400 feet high on a base of 100 feet square. An earthquake destroyed it in the 1300's. It was used by seamen for over 1500 years. To most of the people in the world, the pharaoh in Alexandria symbolized the power and glory in the Greek nations. The greatest of the city named after Alexander was the city on the Mediterranean cost of Egypt, where the pharos of Greek origin got many magnificent construction.

After Alexander had left, his general Ptolemy 1 became its ruler (pharaoh). His family ruled Egypt for 300 years. Beauty queen Cleopatra was the last of his dynasty. During this period. This city became the center of world's trade and learning. Alexander the Great had the idea of building a library. Keeping his master's vision in view, Ptolemy 1 appointed Soustratus as the architect and started the work on it. This lighthouse was completed during the reign of Ptolemy 2 (309-246 BC).

It was built on a base of 100 ft. square. A walled platform around the base of the lighthouse protected it from the sea. Drinking water was supplied by an aqueduct and was stored in the base of the building. There were hundreds of rooms leading to the ramp. These had outward facing window and used to keep watch out at sea. Astronomers also used these windows for experiments. The upper part of the lighthouse was reached by a slopping spiral ramp. The fire at the top, to warn the ships at night, was said to be a pillar of fire by night and smoke by day. Fuel for the fire was carried up in a horse drawn cart. Then hoisted to the top by pulleys. The light of fire was reflected out to sea by an enormous concave mirror. Crowning the very top of the mirror was a statue of Helios.

It remained a world wonder for 1500 years. Even Saint Paul had described its splendor. In 1300 AD, a powerful earthquake destroyed it. In the following years, the seas engulfed the ruins. This wonder of the world was lost forever. In 1993, salvage operation divers found several its pieces near the coast on Alexandria. In 2003, with the help of Sonar and underwater cameras, it has been discovered that the ruins are lying in the depth of the Mediterranean, some 3-4 km away from the coast.

The Great Buddhas:

Buddhism is one of the oldest religions in the world. It was founded in India by Siddharth Gautham, a Prince who became the Buddha-the enlightened one. By third century BC, Buddhism had become the main religion in Asia. Today, almost 250 million throughout the world follow it. Buddha's statues have been built since 3rd century BC. Today, there are thousands of huge images of Buddha.

In Afghanistan, there was a huge statue carved out of the mountains. It was built some 2,400 years ago. It was more than 100 ft tall. In it, Buddha was standing. These world heritage statues were destroyed by fanatic Muslims in 2000 AD. There is 10th century figure of Buddha in the city of Pegu, Burma known as Shwethalyaung, the colossal statue is 18- ft long and 46 ft high at shoulders. After Pegu was destroyed in 1757, the city was gradually overrun by jungles. The Shwethalyaung lay hidden for a century, until it was discovered by chance in 1881. In was enclosed in an iron pavilion in 1906 and renovated in 1946.

In Thailand, a magnificent 60 ft high figure of Buddha is seated on a pedestal inside Wattrimitr (Temple of Golden Buddha). It is made of 5.5 tons of solid gold and is the most valuable statue in the world. To conceal its priceless value, the statue was covered in a layer of plaster. This 13th century statue remained in this state until 1953. Its true nature was only revealed when the statue was dropped, and the plaster cracked.

Also, in Bangkok, there is a huge statue of Reclining Buddha. It is gold plated. In the same complex, another very costly statue is the Emerald Buddha. There lies a 13th century Granite Buddha in a secluded spot in the forest near Polonnaruwa in Sri Lanka. In Galvihar Temple, there are four huge statue depicted in different poses; two are seated and one is lying down, while the last is standing. China also has a very tall statue of Buddha: it is more than 150 ft.

Moai: Easter Island

A mere 40 sq mile in extent, totally secluded from other islands of pacific and mainland, Easter Island is located some 2,300 miles of west of Chile. (Now part of it since 1888). Suddenly making headlines when an English woman named Katherine Routledge, it was discovered to have hundreds of weird stone statues with all sorts of expressions. The first European explorer, Jacob Roggeveen, set for on this island in 1772. He saw these fallen statues but did not give it much care. Of course, he sighted the island on Easter Sunday, thus naming it. Its ancient name was Te-Pito-Tehenua, thus meaning 'navel of the world'.

After the discovery, wide interest and curiosity brought researchers to the spot. They found it a place of surging breakers, precipitous cliffs, towering volcanos, and open windswept slopes. Dominating the landscapes were the famous statues, who's heads immense, their expressions brooding and distasteful, ear elongated, chins jutting and powerful, arms hanging rigidly at the sides of their legless trunks, hands expanding stiffly across their bellies. Almost 1,000 such statues of buff colored volcanic stone (some weighing 20 tons and 12-15 ft tall), the largest weighing 90 tons. They also found some unfinished statues, more than twice the size of this colossus.

Now the million-dollar questions? Who made them and why? What happened to the men who carved the? How were the statues moved from the quarries, and raised on their altars (Ahu)? Some altars are 200 yards long, 20 feet high, and 6-15 ft high with walls of unmortised stone s (like Inca stonework). The researchers have guessed that the islanders were cannibals. Class warfare, intense competition among kin groups, over population and depleting resources forced a civil war. They people became victims and they were brought down. By 19th century, all had been brought down; Europeans made most of them slaves. In 1877, there were only 187 natives.

Researchers further found out that the statues were hewn out of a close-grained volcanic tuff from the slopes of the satellite volcano, Ranoraraka, on the eastern part of the island. Still, there are 300 statues on that side. Most of the Ahu on which they once stood are found near the shores of the island.

Local tradition maintains that Hotumatu, a Polynesian chief, came here with his people from Hiva Island, before 690 AD. They developed civilizations, thus proved by carbon dating. The earliest altar was made from 1,110 to 1,105 AD. Some classical statues were made till 1650 AD.

How the Moai, statues were transported and raised, is the most perplexing question. Some believe it is the result is slave labor, which disappeared in later days. Local tradition believes in supernatural powers called the Mana, with Moai. They simply walked and sat on the platform. Some believe that volcanic eruption slipped them down, placing them on the altars. Some locals still believe that vast carpets of sweet potatoes and crushed yams were laid on slopes, and statues were slid along them to altars.

Researchers still maintain that the entire truth about Easter Island's coast may remain shrouded in mystery for a long time to come.

Stonehenge:

On Salisbury Plains in Southern England is one of the most ancient standing stone monuments, we know nothing of the people who built it, but they must have possessed sophisticated technology given the complexity of this structure. Why these structures were made of huge stones, sometimes transported from hundreds of miles? The alignment of the stones may have been important in the observation of the stars and eclipses. This may be the purpose of Stonehenge. Here, each stone in the giant double circle weighs more than 50 tons. These stones were transported from two quarries: one was about 12 miles (20 km) from the sight, the other at 120 m (200 km). This is a circle of megaliths (huge stones). It was certainly one of the most important monuments of its time. This gigantic stone structure was erected some 5,000 years ago, towards the end of the Stone Age.

It has been modified several times in the 1,500 years that followed. The outer circle, more than 100 ft (30 m) in diameter is composed of enormous single stones, topped by linking stone slabs. The inner circle consists of smaller stones. At the center are five pairs of vertical stones, each supporting the horizontal block. Just outside the circle stands the Heel stone, which aligns with a point on the horizon, where the sun rises on Midsummer Day. Perhaps they were used for some worship and other Pagan religious ceremonies and astronomical observations.

Guardians of the Tomb:

As far back as 10th century BC, Chinese rulers built themselves magnificent tombs on the outskirts of their capital cities. These tombs were filled with royal treasures. Statues were built to guard these treasures and the soul of the emperor, as his body was taken to the tomb. These Guardians of the Tomb have been found in the tomb of the first emperor of the Ming dynasty, who ruled some 2,000 years ago.

In 1974, peasants digging a well near the city of Xi'an in Northwest China, came across the thousands of life size terracotta warriors that had been standing guard by the tomb of Emperor Qin Shi Huangdi. This first emperor of the Ming rules for 36 years in 3rd century BC. His tomb was built as an underground 'imperial' city, with a throne room and treasure houses. Archaeologists have not yet excavated the tomb, but in three underground vaults, about 2 km from the tomb, the terracotta army was found.

Some 8,000 statues of soldiers, some with horses and chariots, grouped in battle order stood in attention. Made in pottery, the figures are about six feet tall on average, and hollow with solid arms and legs. The heads and hands were modeled separately. Each figure has different features and expressions and wears marks of rank. Lining the avenue are massive statues of animals. Up to 12 feet tall, each made with a simple block of blue limestone. There are 24 pairs of animals in all on either side of the road: lions, camels, horses, elephants, and mythological beasts. After passing through the animals, one comes to 12 colossus statues of Chinese officials called 'Manadrins'. Some represent the emperor's personal soldiers. Dressed in long coats of armor and close-fitting helmets, they carry swords or batons and look very fierce.

Ellora Rock:

Nowhere will one find such marvels of rock carving and architecture as in Ellora, a sickle shaped hill about 30 km from Aurangabad in Maharashtra, India. The cave carving started in 450 AD and ended in 650 AD. Started by Buddhists, Hindu and Jains were known to join them; there, one finds caves of all three religions. Out of 34 carved caves, 12 to the south are Buddhist, 17 are of Hindus and 5 belong to Jains. All have been dug into the sloping side of the hill. Only chisel and small hammers were used. In each of the Buddhist caves, there is one prayer hall with monasteries attached. Some of they have a height of 50 feet. The three storied caves mark the climax of the rock architecture achievements. Largest of them is Cave 5; its big prayer hall contains 24 pillars. In the next one, two remarkable statues attract the visitor: a large seated Buddha and a standing figure of Saraswati (Goddess of Learning). Cave 10 and 12 are marked for their wonderful carvings and finely embellished interior. In almost all 17 caves, there are statues of Buddha in all poses. These depict his life and Jataka tales.

Most of the Hindu caves were carved out in the 7th and 8th century. Their workmanship is better, and one finds a true depiction of Hindu mythology in quite dramatic and dynamic design. All of them were carved down from the top to floor- a feat most outstanding and unmatched in the reams of rock architecture and cave temples. Cave 14 has the carvings of lord Shiva, lord Vishnu, Goddess Durga, Goddess Lashio and several others who matter in Hindu mythology. The body and facial expressions show how the artists brought the best out of themselves. Cave 15 depicts all ten incarnations of Vishnu. It is one of the best caves of Ellora, with fine reliefs inside the upper story.

The best Cave is said to be 16; it has been carved out from one single rock with a gateway, pavilion courtyard, prayer hall, vestibule, sanctum sanctorum with a huge tower called Kalash temple- abode of Lord Shiva. Its size is fantastic: 267 ft in length, 154 ft in width, and 107 ft in depth. It has been regarded world's greatest monolithic wonder, with an awe-inspiring execution. In the center, there is the main temple which is supported by elaborately sculptured friezes of elephants. In the galleries, there are wonderful panels conducted to the legends of Lord Shiva and Lord Vishnu, especially the gigantic Nursing (Man-Lion tearing the body of Demon Hiranyakashyapa). On the pillar, Ravan the demon king is shown trying to shake Mount Kailash, with Lord Shiva putting his toe down on the mountain so hard that Ravana's hand getting crushed under the might. Ravana's anguish is visible, as Parvati, consort of Shiva, looks down somewhat perturbed.

The Jain caves are a bit more modest yet detailed in design and execution. In Cave 32, Indrasabha is outstanding. Here, the king of Gods is the finest. There are statues of lord Mahavir, Parshunath and the other 22 Thirtankar of Jain faith. These caves are one of the greatest heritages of mankind.

Ajanta- a rock retreat:

Ajanta is another world heritage site with Ellora. These caves are 105 km away from Aurangabad and run in the sickle shaped curve along the face of cliffs for about 2 km. There are 29 cave temples and monasteries of different sizes. They are much older than that of Ellora. Began in 200 BC, the caves continued being built till about 200 AD. Viharas (monasteries of Ajanta) have an additional dimension in the form of large numbers of mural frescoes, which have survived even after 2,000 years, some fully intact. These paintings depict the contemporary life, culture, and traditions alongside stories of Buddha's life. This treasure of unprecedented maturity of colors, wonderful postures and positions is awe-inspiring.

4 of 29 caves are shrines (Chaityas). The rest of the caves are monasteries. Cave 1 has the paintings of Bodhisattwa with blue lotus and other frescoes, including Sibijatak. Cave 2 is devoted to the final incarnation of Buddha, the dream of queen May and the nativity of Siddharth, the real name of Buddha. Cave 16 is also related to Buddha's birth. In these paintings, one finds an outstanding combination of figures with architectural motifs. Cave 17 contains the largest number of frescoes. All of them depict the life of Buddha. Cave 16 and 17 were made under Wakatak rulers.

They have pillared halls, with statues of seated Buddha. Cave 4 is the example of fine sculpture. It has the largest monastery. One can find Chaityas, shrines, quite overwhelming in size and dimensions in Cave 10. However, the paintings in this cave have been damaged badly. Cave 1, 2,16,17,19 is famous for their mural frescoes. Cave 1, 4,17,19,26 is famous for their predominance of sculptures. This setting, workmanship, and artistic creativity have set standards for all times.

Hagia Sophia:

The Roman Empire's buildings in Rome thrill everyone, even to date. The Eastern Roman empire, with its capital at Constantinople (now Istanbul) has a marvelous monument of the Byzantine: the Hagia Sophia, a great architectural beauty and a monument both for Byzantine and Ottoman Empires. Once a church, later a Mousk, now a museum, it has been precious.

Today, Istanbul carries characteristics of both Byzantine and Ottoman cultures. Hagia Sophia is a perfect synthesis; people can observe the effects of both cultures under one great dome. This world-famous monument, located in Sultan Mahmet square of Istanbul, was built with ashlar and bricks. It is 82 m (269 ft) long and 73 m (240 ft) wide, with a huge dome at the height of 55 m (180 ft). Its construction took five years from 532 AD to 537 AD, under orders from Emperor Justinian.

It is said that Hagia Sophia was built on the site of an ancient temple used by Roman Emperor's prior to their embrace of Christianity. It underwent two phases of construction before its present shape. The first construction was started by Emperor Constantias, son of Constantine I. It was opened for service in 360 AD, as an orthodox church. At that time, it was a basilica type structure, with a rectangular floor plan. It had circles apes and a timbered roof. Constantias donated precious articles and released objects to it. It was named Megaleekkiesia (The Great Church), as it was the largest church in Constantinople. Later, it was named Sophia (the name symbolizes the second divine attribute of the holy trinity).

The original church was destroyed in 404 AD, by mob when Emperor Arcadius sent the Petrarch of Constantinople in exile for criticizing the Queen. Emperor Theodeus built a new church to be completed in 415 AD, on the design of Ruffinos. On October 25 986, it was destroyed by an earthquake. Repairs finished in 994. In 1204, the church was sacked by fourth crusaders. Emperor Michael 8 (1261-1282). In 1370, south-western walls were reinforced on the exterior by pyramid shaped buttresses.

After 1453, it was converted into a mosque. Sultan Ahmed 2 the conqueror built an altar in the east apse, Sultan Bayezid (1484-1512), added minarets on the northeastern corridor. The Turkish architect Sinan built the two minarets in front of the church in the reign of Sultan Murad 3 (1574-1635). He also brought water urns of 300 BC from Bergama. During the reign of Murad 4, pulpit and priests' pew were added to the interior. In 1739, Sultan Mahmud built a library. In 1850, the present-day imperial pew was added.

In 1926, the government of the New republic appointed a technical commission to investigate the architectural and static state of the building thoroughly. Following the order Mustafa Kemal Pasha, Ataturk, Hagia Sophia was converted to a museum on February 1, 1935.

Since then, this architectural wonder remains a conglomerate of east and west: Roman and Turkish, Christianity and Islam, attracting millions every year.

CHAPTER FIVE

New Wonders of The World

The greatest poll of its kind, led by Canadian-Swiss Bernard Weber and organized by Swiss based government controlled New Wonder Forum, with Weber, announced on July 7, 2007 in Lisbon the names of the New 7 Wonders of the World. More than 100 million people all over the world have participated in voting. **The New Wonders are Taj Mahal, the Great Wall of China, Coliseum of Rome, Petra, Machu Picchu, Statue of Christ the Redeemer and Chickenitza**

Taj Mahal:

The Taj Mahal, one of the buildings of the medieval world, is the most beautiful Mausoleum in the world today. It stands at the banks of river Jamuna, on the banks of Agra. It was built by the Mughal Emperor Shah Jahan in memory of his beloved wife Mumtaz Mahal (meaning 'Pride of the Palace'). When she died giving birth to their ninth child, the inconsolable emperor decided to build a Mausoleum of such perfect beautify to immortalize his love for her. Work started in 1632 AD and completed in 1640 AD. 20,000 masons and artists worked under the direct supervision of several architects. Chief among the architects was the Persian Shirazi. "Taj Mahal' means crown of palace in Persian. It is built of white marble, and rests on an eight-sided platform of red sandstone. Each side is 130 ft long. At each corner of the platform stands a slender prayer tower, or Minaret. These Minarets are 133 ft high. The building itself is 186 ft sq. A beautiful tomb dome covers the center part of the building. The inside is inlaid with 43 types of precious stone, including sapphire, jade, and crystal. This dome is 70 ft in diameter, and 120 ft high. Passages from the holy Koran decorate the outside. A central room contains two monuments. the bodies of the royal couple lie in a vault below the room. The inside is lighted by delicate carved stone. Surrounded by formal gardens, it rises at the end of a long pool in which its image is reflected. Today, several million local and foreign tourists visit this poem in marble.

The Great Wall of China:

The Great Wall of China was built mainly in the 3 century BC, and extensively restored in 14 century AD. It is said to be visible from the moon. In 221 BC, Emperor Qin Shih Hongi decided to strengthen the rampart parts of northern China, as protection against barbarians. To do so, he joined preexisting sections of wall together to make it a continuous 1850 mi (3000 km) barrier. Many of the 300,000 men assigned to the task died while working on it. The resulting wall, between 20 and 60 ft high, snaked through the hills defining the northern part of China for many centuries. A road on the top of the wall facilitated the movement of horsemen and chariots between small forts built at regular intervals along it. Abandoned for several centuries, the wall was restored by Ming rulers.

It is the largest man-made construction in the world. Built along the crest of a mountain range, the wall formed an effective barrier against fierce tribes and other invaders. Guards who were posted along the wall sounded the alarm if there was danger. This construction shows that people in the east were greatly expertized in huge construction of this time. Westerners did not know about it till the 14th or 15th century.

The Coliseum of Rome:

Coliseum is an amphitheater at Rome. The word comes from the Latin word 'Colossus', which means gigantic. The Coliseum was named for a huge statue of Emperor Nero, which stood nearby. The other amphitheaters were also called by that name. The Coliseum is one of the most beautiful ruins of the world. The ruins rise to a height of four stories on one side. It was begun by Vespasian and finished by Domination in 82 AD. Some 20,000 slaves worked on it. It was oval and measured about 650 ft long, 510 ft wide and 150 ft high. There were seats for 50,000 spectators who were seated according to social rank, arranged in sections to the left and right of the imperial box. In the event of rain, a velarium was stretched over the arena, the central place. Men and animals fated to participate in spectacles were kept in cells beneath the arena and were hoisted into it by an elevator worked by weights and pulleys. In 249 AD, to celebrate the 1000 anniversary of the city's founding, the most incredible and blood thirsty spectacle took place. Some 2,000 gladiators took part and during combat 32 elephants, 10 giraffes, 60 lions and 10 tigers were killed. Not to talk of the number of gladiators. The Coliseum was well preserved until the 500s AD. Then, for 100 years, its stones were used for other buildings. The building was saved from complete destruction by Pope Benedict 14 in 1700s. Today it tells the tale of glory that was Rome.

Machu Picchu:

South America also had vibrant civilizations capable of producing beautiful things. One of them was developed by the Incas and destroyed by Spanish conquistador Francisco Pizzaro and his follower's through deceit, treachery and cunning. This process started in 1532 AD, with the deceitful arrest of the Inca ruler Atahualpa. He paid Pizzaro the most fabulous ransom in recorded history. Greedy Spaniards still executed him. Consequently, his successors and followers retreated to safer resorts. Where remained a mystery till 1911, when an American explorer Hiram Bingham finally traced out the city of Machu Picchu with help of his hill guide Arteaga.

Sat 7,000 up the Andes in the cedar of the hills above the Urubamba River, the first view of the city looks like a great flight of beautifully constructed stone face terraces. The walls of ruined houses have been built by the finest quality of Inca stonework. There is a cave lined with the finest cut stones. Perhaps this serves a royal mausoleum; above it is a semicircular building whose outer walls follow the natural curator of the rock. It is keyed to the rock by the finest example of masonry. Not only this temple, but the whole city is made with granite stone which came from the quarry at the top of the mountain. This shows that the work is still on. The city is so well preserved that only the reed and straw roofs need to be replaced to bring the city to life again. Some 300 houses on the mountain terraces produce a beautiful special.

Every house has a window facing the east, so that sunlight graces the houses in the morning. There is a carved stone, supposedly sacred, which is said to be an Incan altar. This was meant for some worship. Each year, during winter, solstice in June (when the sun is at its lowest point in the sky) the high priests symbolically bound the Sun God Inti into the stone with golden chain to make sure that he returned for the southern hemisphere's summer. This prison shaped pillar was also used as a sun dial. Beneath this tower is a royal mausoleum, one of the strangest monuments of Inca art. Its walls are faced with finely worked stone slabs. A throne at several alcoves is cut out of solid rock. All the buildings have been built by placing one stone atop another. It is a wonder that no mortar has been used anywhere. It is guessed that Machu Picchu was constructed during the reign of Pachacuti Inca, who ruled in the first half of the 15 century. He has been exported as the greatest man that the aboriginal race of America has produced. In his times, the city might have served as a military garrison, protecting the northern flank of Cuzco, capital of Incan empire, from hostile tribes who inhabited the upper Amazon basin. It was also used in the following century as a sanctuary for the virgins of the Sun, to save them from the Spaniards' lust. Even today, one can see a system of paved streets cut into steps because of the city's sloping side. Machu Picchu has opened a new vista in the history of civilization.

Petra:

Petra was once a thriving city in the heart of the desert, some 150 km southwest of Amman, capital city of modern-day Jordan. Ancient authors have written a lot about the city. It remained undiscovered, however, for centuries. It was suddenly discovered in 1812, when Swiss adventurer John Ludwig Burkhardt was guided through a narrow deep gorge to some astounding ruins. The hill had been carved into facades of palaces or temples in Greek style. This was the old forgotten city of Petra- a rose red city half as old as time. A door in each facade opening into a corridor provided access to an empty room carved out of rock. This might have served as an altar for worship. In the 4th century BC, a race known as Nabataea Arabs made Petra their home. Soon, it became a big city at an important caravan crossing route. The Nabataens were clever people and understood the importance of the crossing. They levied tolls on goods passing through. This revenue made them rich, and hence more development of Petra.

The holy place of the city was at the top of the mountain peak, which could be reached by stairway cut into rock. This sanctuary is still unharmed. There is a platform 45 ft by 20 ft. It is said that it was once covered by gold. A sacrificial altar in the form of a block of sandstorm lays on four steps. This stands out on the platform.

With the rise of the Roman Empire, Nabataens had to forgo their independence. Thus, their decline began. Petra's prosperity, however, sustained until caravans began taking other routes. Several invasions finally sent the city into oblivion.

Statue of Christ the Redeemer:

It is wonderful to see how religious fever can create a world wonder. Even in the 20th century. The Statue of Christ the Redeemer, in Brazil Rio De Janner, is a glaring example. It is the largest Deco statue in the world. It stands 39.6 meters (139 ft tall), including 9.5 meters (31 ft) pedestal. It is 30 meters (98 ft) wide and includes His all-embracing outstretched hands. The entire statue weight 635 tons. Located at the peak of 700 meters (2,300 ft), Corcovado Mountains in Tijuca Forest National Park, the statue overlooks the city is the icon of Rio and Brazil. It is made of reinforced concrete and coated with soap stone.

The idea of a Christian monument was first suggested in the middle of 1850s, when Catholic priest Pedrowaria Boss requested financing from Princess Isabelle of Portugal to build a large religious memorial. For some time, the princess pondered over the proposal before rejecting it in 1889, when Brazil became independent and the church was separated from the state. The second proposal came from the Catholic circle of Rio in 1921. A signature campaign and fundraising drive started. Several designs, including a Christian Cross, Statue of Christ with glove in hands and a pedestal symbolizing the world, and the present one was considered. Finally, Christ the Redeemer was selected. Local engineer Heitor DaSilva Costa and French sculptor Paul Landowska worked on it. The construction began in 1922, and statue was constructed nine years later. The cost was $250,000. The opening ceremony was held on October 12, 1931. This marked a great religious fervor. Originally, it was meant to be lit by a battery of flood lights triggered remotely by short wave radio designed by pioneer Guglielmo Marconi. Marconi was stationed in Rome at the time. After some time, bad weather affected the signal and the statue had to be lit by workers in Rio.

The statue's 75 anniversary was celebrated in October 2006. The archbishop of Rio, Eusebio Oscar Sheld, consecrated a chapel under the statue in the honor of Nossa San Hora Apareuda (the patron saint of Brazil). This allowed Catholics to hold baptisms and weddings there.

On Sunday, February 10, 2008, the statue was hit by lightning due to violent electrical storms. This caused some damage to the fingers, head, and eyebrows. The restoration work was put in by Rio State Government and Archdiocese. On April 5, 2010 somebody sprayed graffiti on the statue's head and right arm. Mayor Adarado Paes called the act antinational and vowed to punish the vandals. He also offered a reward of $10,000 for information about the vandals. They are still at large.

Chickenitza:

Along with Egypt, China and India, Mexico can also boast of flourishing civilization in ancient times. Recent researches have shown that Maya civilization was as great as that of China and Asia. it has been estimated that in Mexico alone, there are 100,000 monuments still hidden in rich jungles. Out of them, the pyramid of El Castillo, appearing as the colonnade of the temple of warriors, is the best preserved and the greatest architectural achievement of Chickenitza. It was built by fierce ruler Tolteches. El Castillo, as the name suggests, appears to be a castle, but not so; in fact, it's a temple. Its four symmetrical staircases on all four sides have 365 steps to the top. They symbolize the number of days in a year. Mayans were very much obsessed by time. Hence, this number of steps. It has been built to a square plan. The total height of this pyramid is 78 ft. It is made up of two superimposed pyramids. The whole structure is built in stone. It does not have an apex like Egyptian pyramids, which were built as tombs for pharos. It is solely built as a gigantic base for miniscule temples. It can be compared to the Ziggurats of the Mesopotamia. The temple at the top of the pyramid would bring Mayans nearer to their Gods.

The pyramid has steps fit into it, up which the priests and those intended for sacrifice ascended to the temple. Other worshippers had to stare up at the ceremonies from ground level. The main purpose of the pyramid was to enable the high priests to meet the god of the Mayas.

CHAPTER SIX

Natural Wonders of The World

Old Faithful Geyser:

Geyser is a spring which throws up hot water with explosive force from time to time. Often, the water is shot up in great columns, cloudy with steam. In volcanic regions, molten lava heats up the Earth's crust, causing boiling water to shoot up from underground. This occurs, for example, at Lake Bogoria in Kenya and at geyser Flut near Rotorua in New Zealand. However, some of the most spectacular geysers are in Yellowstone National Park in Wyoming, which can boast having 84 geysers. The most famous of them is Old Faithful.

For more than 100 years, it has shot water and vapor up to 100 ft into the air, 23 times a day. Most of the times it takes 65 minutes interval. On two occasions, its eruptions were only 33 minutes apart. Once it waited 91 minutes. The heights of eruptions are usually 120-150 ft. There are other geysers of equal importance in this park. The highest is 'Steamboat'. It can project steam and water to heights of more than 300 ft. Splashing boiling and whistling noises accompany them. Deposits left buy the water from them often take an attractive or unusual form. Liberty Cap geyser was once a mammoth hot springs. It is now inactive. For many years, hot water and steam spouted up out of the Earth, leaving mineral deposits with built up cone shaped column. The cone is 30 ft high and has a base of 20 ft diameter. There is an opening at the top of the cone.

Largest Volcano:

For hundreds of years volcanoes have struck terror and wonder into the heart of man. In ancient times they even moved man to worship them. A volcano is an opening in the Earth's surface. Through this opening has come rock so hot that it is in liquid or gaseous state. The world's largest volcano is Mauna Kea, Hawaii. Its diameter is more than 60 miles (100 km) and its overall height is 13,483 ft. Lava from Mauna Kea covers an area of more than 2,300 sq mi. At night, a view of the fire pit of Mauna Kea presents a natural fireworks display. The surface of the lava is black. From time to time molten rocks from underneath explode upwards in a fountain of fiery sparks. The stream of red-hot lava continuously flows into the sea, thus gaining land. The sea water at these points is always at a boiling point. Hawaii consists of some 20 volcanic islands, which owe their existence to a hot point in the Earth's mantle.

Due to volcanic activity, much of the Hawaiian archipelago is covered with solidified lava and is uninhabitable. Other famous volcanoes in the world are Vesuvius (Italy), Etna, Stromboli (Sicily), Fuji (Japan), Krakatoa (Indonesia), Kilimanjaro (Tanzania), Chaune-des-puis (France). Most of these are inactive.

In April 2010, a volcanic eruption on Iceland threw air services out of gear. Life in half of the world, especially in Europe, was left paralyzed.

Grand Canyon:

A canyon is a deep valley, or gorge, carved out by a river over thousands of years. As a river flows, it wears away the riverbed near it. The Grand Canyon in Arizona USA is the most famous canyon in the world. Here the Colorado has worn away the solid rock to make a canyon 280 mi (450 km long). In some places, the canyon is more than 6,000 ft (1,800 m) deep and 18 miles (29 km) wide. As one descends into the crater, one sees the exposed layers of rock from different prehistoric ages. This gives us fascinating information about the past.

For 65 million years the waters of the Colorado River have worn away the rock of a desert plateau, carving a huge chasm. Created almost entirely by the action of flowing water, the Grand Canyon is the largest gorge in the world. Differences in the resistance of various stone to erosion have created a variety of slopes and counters, massive screes, and towering perpendicular walls. 2 billion years of the Earth's history are inscribed on the canyon's multicolored stratified walls, which are a corridor through geological time. Only the gorges of the Yangtze River in China rival its spectacular grandeur and beauty.

At sunrise and sunset, one can see the rocks changing colors. The best view of the canyon can be seen through an air flight, which takes tourists just above the Colorado River, which appears to be a thin thread from the plane. Some of the peaks in the crater have been named as Vishnu Temple and Shiva Temple. This is the largest canyon and natural wonder of the world.

Chain of Lakes:

The USA has thousands of lakes of all shapes and sizes. The Great Lakes make up the largest group of lakes in the country as well as the greatest collection of freshwater lakes in the world. The Great Lakes- Superior, Michigan, Huron, Eerie and Ontario- are situated along the border between the United States and Canada. Connected to the Atlantic Ocean by the Saint Lawrence Seaway, together they are 1,160 miles from east to west. They are the size of an inland sea. These five freshwater lakes came into existence from movements in the Earth's crust that followed the last ice age, creating a series of enormous basins.

With a surface area of 31,400 sq mi (81,350 sq km), Lake Superior is the largest lake in the western hemisphere. It has shores in both the USA and Canada. The landscape around the lake is varied. Ranging from forests to fields and dunes to large open spaces. Several great manufacturing cities have developed in this region. This is one of the most industrialized areas in Northern America. The third largest city and greatest railway center Chicago is on the shores of Lake Michigan. Detroit, the capital of the automobile industry, is near Lake Eerie. Toronto, the greatest city of Canada, lies on the Ontario. Their navigability to the Atlantic has made them the biggest inland waterways of the world.

The Deepest Lake in the World:

Lake Baikal is the largest body of fresh water in Asia. With a maximum depth of 4,870 ft (1,485 m), this lake is situated in the southernmost of Siberia. It is additionally the world's deepest lake. Bays and peninsulas are cut out of the shoreline of the lake, which has an area of 12,000 sq mi. around it are beautiful cliffs and high mountains. This immense reservoir of fresh water freezes over late in the year. Packs of ice exist, however, until July. In summer, high wind waves can rise to a height of 16 ft (5 m). More than 50 species of fish live in its waters. Sturgeon, from whose egg's caviar is prepared, is the best-known fish that lives there.

Mariana's Trench: The Deepest Ocean Canyon:

The Pacific is not only the biggest ocean but also contains the lowest and deepest portions of the Earth. To the east of Mariana Island, there is a deep curving canyon in the floor of the ocean. This is known as Marianna's trench. Discovered by a British oceanographic vessel in 1951, this great submarine canyon is 1,585 mi (2,550 km long) and near 45 mi (70 km) wide. Its deepest point is 36, 00 ft (11, 34 m) below sea level. It is the lowest point of Earth's surface; Explorers have declared it to be an immense emptiness that defies understanding.

Titicaca: The Highest Lake in the World:

The highest lakes are found in the Himalayan region of India. Most of them, however, are frozen year-round. First among them is Panchpokhri, 17,760 ft (5,414 m) above sea level. Hemkund, Roopund, Mansarovar are other such lakes. The highest navigable lake in the world is Lake Titicaca on the borders between Bolivia and Peru in the South American continent. This huge landlocked lake is situated at least 12,507 ft (3,812 m) above sea level and is more than 880 ft (270 m) deep in places. Its area is more than 3000 sq mi (8000 sq km). Like the Mansarovar in Tibet, Lake Titicaca was sacred to people living in the Incan Empire up to the 17th century. As the legend goes, the people of the Andes originated on one of its islands called 'Island of the Sun'. The banks of the lake are thickly with reeds (totoras) which the Andean Indians used for centuries to make boats. In this reed woven boats, they crossed the lake, fished, and traveled to the floating islands (Uros) where some of them lived and cultivated gardens.

Taiga: Largest Forest in the World:

The Taiga- the largest forest on the earth- stretches from Finland in Europe to Japan in Asia, from the Baltic Sea to Pacific Ocean. It covers millions of miles across Siberia in Russia. Finland, Sweden, and European parts of Russia have more than 200,000,000 acres of forest. Russia's Asian part has twice the area of its counterpart in Europe. It offers a landscape in which the only variation is the density of trees. In Siberia at some places they are thin and far from large population centers.

Finland and Sweden are heavily wooded. The supply much of the lumber and wood pulp for the continent of Europe. It is believed that Russia has about 1/3 of the world's timber. The Taiga remains partially unexplored. Composed mainly of Birch and Pine, it is inhabited by moose, reindeer, bear, silver foxes and wolves. To the east live tigers' panthers and lynx. Vegetation here is strange. Dead tree trunks are often seen within living trees and the forest floor is covered with a carpet of moss and lichens.

Amazon Forest: Largest Virgin Forest:

Expect for the Polar Regions, about 16 of every hundred acres of land is covered with productive forest. About 2 of every 3 acres of forest are covered by Russia, British Commonwealth, Brazil, and USA. Forest cover almost 45 out of every hundred acres in South America. The continent can supply its own timber needs to export some lumber. But the ring of the woodman's axe has not been heard often in the heart of the hot and thick Amazon jungle. This amazon basin is a vast forested area that extends for more than 2,300,000 sq mi (6,000,000 sq km) over five countries.

It covers part of Bolivia, Peru Columbia, Venezuela and 2/5 of Brazil. Temperature in the basin remains stable throughout the year ranging from 68 to 82 F (20-28 C). Heavy rains fall here year-round. This rain forest is in effect the world's greatest nature reserve. 1/10 of the planets bird species live in its foliage. More than 2,500 fish have evolved in the Amazon River system. An area the size of Greece has been deforested within the space of 10 years. As a result, many plants and animal species are in danger of extinction, as are the human populations native to the region. It is the largest virgin forest in the world yet is constantly being reduced by excessive deforestation.

The Tallest Trees: Sequoia National Parks:

This national park is located on the western slopes of Sierra Nevada in Central California about 220 mi north of Los Angeles. It includes 601.70 sq mi of land. There is a difference of altitude of over 2 mi from the lowest point in the park to the highest mountain peak. This park is famous for giant Sequoia trees. There are more than 50 groves of these giant trees. These trees grow very tall. Some of them are several thousand years old. Now law forbids the cutting of these trees. Before the law was enacted, one of the largest and oldest trees (which was cut down) dated back to 1,305 BC. Its section is preserved in the National History Museum in New York. The General Sherman Tree maybe 3000-4000 years old. It is supposed to be the oldest and largest living thing on Earth. In age it can be compared to the age of Egyptian pyramids. The other variety of Sequoia is Red Wood. This is also a giant tree. They grow only in mountains near the Pacific Coast of Oregon and California. They have tall trunks, which may be 15-18 feet though and more than 300 ft high in length. The tallest redwood is called 'Founders Tree'- it is 365 m high. It is the tallest tree in the world. These trees grow more rapidly than any only cone bearing tree. 1000 years may be necessary to grow a new tree as large as a tree which may be cut down.

Serengeti National Park:

Serengeti National Park in Tanzania has an area of 5,700 sq mi (15,000 sq km). It is one of the biggest game parks in the world. It also spreads into neighboring Kenya. Together with Tsabo National Park of Kenya on the other side of Mount Kilimanjaro, the highest mountain in Africa (19,340 ft), it makes the largest of all 1,500 game reserves. The whole area lies in the Savannas. This is largest sanctuary of lions, elephants, zebras, giraffes, and many other varieties of the antelope family. The entire area is packed with wilder beasts and animals resembling goats and deer. The annual migration of animals presents a spectacular sight. Millions of animal's march after one another. After a gap of say 500 m, another species migrates as well. Thus, it becomes miles long of crossings. Lions and other predators are at the end. This gives them easy chances to prey on stragglers. This concerted migration takes place between the short grassed Masai steppe and Savanna woodland region near Lake Victoria in direct response to food availability. As the Serengeti dry season progresses, they withdraw to the woodlands until the rains begin again. This is the only place in the world where lions can be seen in prides. Leopards, cheetahs, hyenas, and jackals also follow. Serengeti also supports a great diversity of birds including bastard, falcon, and ostrich. Uncontrolled hunting and poaching have severely reduced the animal population, especially elephant and rhinoceros. Many tourists visit the Serengeti every year. Land rovers and private cars move frequently in the area. It is always advisable to take a guide.

Ngorongoro Crater: Nature's Biggest Zoo:

The most wonderful sight in all of Africa and maybe the whole world is the Ngorongoro Crater in Tanzania. It lies somewhere in the middle of Lake Manyara National Park and Samours of Serengeti. The eastern valley has several volcanoes. Ngorongoro Crater is a volcanic crater. Thousands of years ago the 10,000 feet high volcano burst out and lava spilled all around, creating a 600 m (2,000 ft) deep crater, which is now 17 km across. The area of the crater is approximately 120 sq km. If one stands on a hillock in the middle of the crater, he will find a 2,000 ft high wall all around. There is a tract to take land rovers into the crater. One feels like shivering on the rim. He then feels heat and humidity when on the inside. The Lad Rover first takes the tourist to the lake on the middle of the crater.

From the rim, the water of the lake appears to be pink in color. As soon as the Land Rover reaches the lake, one wonders at the fact at the water is not pink; the presence of millions of flamingos makes it so. Hippos are also found in this lake. It comes out at night only. All five big animals – lions, rhino, elephant, and giraffe- are present in this crater. One can see a lion's family and the Masai family living together at harmony in the crater. Several types of antelopes, wilder beasts and eland are found in big heard. These animals have gotten sued to the tourists; thus, they are not disturbed. One can easily see them in their natural habitat. Guides do not let tourists get down though, as it is dangerous. The visit to the crater takes from 5-6 hours. One wonders how so many animals are living in the area. There is one pass through the northern walls. This pass opens into the Serengeti Park. This is the only way for animals to migrate. It is strange than buffalos never enter the park. There are shrubs and small trees which give shelter to hundreds of varieties of birds. There are hundreds of bigger craters in the world, yet none is as lively as Ngorongoro. It is heaven for wildlife lovers. There are good hotels on the rim and toll operators are doing good business in Kenya and Tanzania

Longest River: Cradle of Civilization:

The Nile is the longest river in the world. It is in Africa and flows 4,135 mi (6,670 km) from its farthest source in Burundi to its delta in Egypt. From Lake Victoria, its largest source, the river passes through desert and swamps, tumbles down fierce waterfalls like Michigan falls, and flows through a narrow fertile valley before forming its triangular delta and emptying into the Mediterranean Sea. The ultimate source of the river remained a mystery until the discovery of its southernmost head street: the Lueironza River in Burundi, in 1947. The two mail arms of the Nile (the Blue Nile rising from the mountains of Ethiopia and the White Nile flowing from Lake Victoria) meet at Khartoum, the capital of Sudan. It is navigable in Sudan and Egypt. Civilization was born along the great banks of this river in Egypt. As early as 5000 BC farmers were planting crops in the rich black soil of the Nile valley, one of the most fertile farming regions of the world. It is the only river in the world which rises near the equator and flows into a temperate zone. In its course, the Nile flows through Burundi, Uganda, Ethiopia, Sudan, and Egypt. The Ashwan Dam, originally built in 1902, control the floods and stores water used to irrigate more than 7 million acres of farmland. This is supposed to be the highest dam in the world. The Nile was always regarded as a fatherly figure. In Vatican City, Rome, the statue of Father Nile is a massive carving representing the power of this mighty African River.

The Suez and Panama Canal: Meeting Point of Seas and Oceans:

Although the USA has the greatest network of navigable canals, the two important canals- Suez and the Panama- have acquired international fame as they are international waterways.

Egyptian Pharaoh Necho (610-595 BC) had dreamed of a canal linking the Mediterranean with the Red Sea. It became a reality in 1869. This canal runs in the north and southern direction, across the Isthmus of Suez. It is 120 mi (195 km) from Port Syed on the Mediterranean to Suez on the Red Sea. The canal was originally 560 ft (170 m) wide and 65 ft (20 m) deep. It shortened the route between England and India by 6,000 miles. It also restored the Mediterranean Sea into its ancient position in Europe of Asiatic trade. The estimated cost of the canal was $100,000,000. It took 10 years for the company to build it. In 1888 an international convention agreed that the canal should be opened on equal terms to ships of all countries, in both peace and war times. In 1949 an agreement between the Suez Canal Company and the Egyptian government provided for the ownership of the canal to be given to Egypt when the company's 99-year lease ended in 1969. In 1956 the canal was nationalized by President Nasser of Egypt. Blocked during the 6-day war between Egypt and Israel in 1967, it remained closed from 1967 until 1974. It has since been enlarging to accommodate supertankers. Today, it is the greatest lifeline of the Maritime world

Civil engineers call the Panama Canal 'The Big Ditch'. It is their own way of saying that this is the greatest canal man has ever made and one of the world's greatest engineering feats. This waterway extends for 50.72 miles (80 km) from Limon Bay in the Caribbean Sea on the Atlantic Side to the Bay of Panama in the Pacific. The depth is 40 ft (12 m) in addition to the engineering problems presented by digging the canal through jungles, mountains and swampy land, medical science had to discover new methods of conquering the yellow fever disease, before the canal could be completed. The work on the canal, which had been conceived over 4 centuries ago by the first Spanish explorers was begun by Ferdinand D 'Lesseps in 1880. American engineers completed it in 1914. After working for nine years the French Panama Canal Company was surrounded by a political scandal and the work had to be stopped. USA obtained the administration of the Canal Zone in 1903 and completed the work. This canal saves ships the long passage around South America and circumnavigating Cape Horn- 7,873 mi. About 240000000 of Earth was excavated to build the 'Great Ditch'. This is sufficient to erect 5 ft thick and 10 ft high wall around the world. Now more than 5,000,000 cubic yards of mud is dredged from the canal each year to keep the canal clear. The liner Premen was the biggest ship to pass through the canal before 1940. It paid a toll of $15,143. Since 1914l the Panama Canal has formed the center of Naval and Air defense for the greater part of Northern America. During the first and second world wars ships bearing war materials found the canal the nearest route to the centers of the conflict.

The Largest Rock:

Australia is said to be the smallest continent but can surprisingly boast to have the largest rock in the world. It is 'Uluru' (Ayers Rock) in northern Australia about 280 mi (450 km) southwest of Alice Springs. The visible part of the rock rises to a height of 1,175 ft (358 m) but, like an iceberg, the part that cannot be seen is much larger: plunging 6,890 ft (2,100 m) below the ground this rock is one single piece of stone. It is a reddish-brown color. It is thought to be 600 million years old. Storm drains which tumble in cascades from the rock maintain a ring of green around it. The rock changes colors in the changing light of the sun, glowing spectacularly in the evening when lit by the setting sun. It gives the same view as one enjoys in the Grand Canyon in the USA.

The Himalayas: the highest mountain:

The Himalaya is the highest mountain in the world. The name of The Himalaya comes from the Sanskrit language, meaning 'House of Snow', or 'Snow Range'. The mountains extend in a 1,500-mile curve across southern Asia from the Pamirs, west of the great bend of the Indus river, eastward to the great bend of the Brahmaputra river. They form a barrier which separate the northern plateau of India from Tibet. Parts of The Himalayas range are as much as 200 miles wide. Mount Everest, the highest peak, lies between Tibet and Nepal. At 29,029 ft (8,898 m), it can be regarded as the world's highest peak, if the volcanos of Hawaii are excluded, since the summit of Mauna Kea rises 33,481 ft (10,205 m) from the floor of the Pacific Ocean. It was named after a British Military Engineer, Sir George Everest, who became the surveyor general of India. In 1987, American expedition to Mount K2 in Pakistan challenged Everest's title as the highest peak. Their satellite survey gave K2's altitude as nearly 29,200 ft (8,900 m). Late that year, a research counsel in Rome concluded that Everest was higher. In 1953, Edmund Hilary and Sherpa Tenzing Norgay became the first climbers to reach its summit. Since then more than 500 climbers have made it to the top. The Himalaya has the big and holy lake Mansarovar, which is thought to be the origin of the Indus, Ganges, and Brahmaputra River. Mount Kailash is also thought to be the home of Lord Shiva; thousands visit the shrines every year.

The Great Rift Valley:

One of the world's most distinct topographical; features lies in Africa. It is the Great Rift Valley. This is a giant trough that cuts into the high plateaus and extends from the Dead Sea in the Middle East southward to Mozambique and Swaziland, almost 4,300 mi (6,900 km). The northern section is filled by the Red Sea, between Africa and Arabia. The central section cuts through Ethiopia and divides near Lake Rudolph, or Turkana, into branches: the western rift arcs through Uganda to Lake Masa (Lake Malawi) and is occupied by Lakes Albert, Edward, Kevu and Tanganyika. The eastern rift cuts through Kenya and Tanzania and joins the western rift near Lake Myasa. In places the rift valley walls rise more than 3,200 m above the flat and sometimes drowned valley floor. One can see both the walls near Arusha, Tanzania and enjoy the beautiful scenery on its floor. Two of the rocky plates that make up the Earth's crust are moving apart, causing some of the Earth's mantle to collapse. This threatens, eventually, to divide Africa into two. This great fissure visible from spacecraft's 80,000 mi (13530 km) from Earth is caused by underground forces that have torn the Earth's crust, resulting in volcanic upheavals and lava eruptions. Some 30 active volcanoes, together with Sulfur springs which are changing lakes into sands, indicate that this process is very much alive. Each year the two sides of the rift are pulled a few inches farther apart.

Channel Tunnels:

The English Channel is an arm of the sea which separates France and England. The French call the channel La Manche, meaning the sleeve. This is one of the most important waterways in the world. It is about 350 mi long and varies in width from 100 miles at the widest point to 20 mi at the narrowest place between Dover England and Calais France. Geologists believe that England and France were once connected by land. Before the channel was formed. During the Second World War the rough waters of the English Channel kept away the German armies from invading

England. With the establishment of European community, it became imperative on England and France to make a tunnel under the channel connecting the narrowest points. With the benefits of modern technology, it became possible. The work began in 1986 and completed in 1994. It was bored through the bed of the English Channel at a depth varying between 18 and 150 ft (25 and 45 meters). The channel tunnel is in fact not one but three tunnels! Two of these contain rail tracks for trains that carry passengers, vehicles, and goods. The third act as a maintenance and service tunnel. Specially designed trains take 35 minutes to travel the 30 miles (50 km) separating Falkstone and Calais. With this tunnel Britain no longer remains an island. The success of this tunnel inspired the Japanese to connect their main islands by such tunnels. They did so. Now, some people are dreaming of making tunnels across the Atlantic Ocean to connect Europe and America by train.

The Largest Desert:

The word desert evokes an arid landscape where the sun scorches the sand, and nothing grows. In some regions water evaporates as soon as it rains. Since there is only 8 in (20 cm) of rain a year in those places nothing can grow. 1/5 of the Earths landmass can be called desert. They are found on all continents. The Sahara in North Africa is the largest sand and stone desert. It has an area of more than 3500000 sq mi (9000000 sq mi. The greatest dimensions of the Sahara are approximately 3,200 mi (5,150 km) from east to west and 1,400 (2,250 km) from north to south. Altitude ranges from 433 (132 m) below sea level in the Qattara depression in Egypt to 11,205 ft (3, 415 m) above sea level at mountain Kaussi in Chad. The temperature can rise to more than 113 F (45 C) at noon and falls below freezing at night. Its sand is highly mobile: a high wind can transform an entire landscape. The world's tallest sand dunes can be seen here at Issouame N'Tifeinine in Algeria. They are 3 mi (5 km) long and over 1,500 ft (450 m) high. They are referred to as sand seas. Now a days, the Sahara is an enormous salt hollow called a Choti. There was once a time when the Sahara was wet. The changes that took place are due to climactic changes that guided the whole Earth. For several years the Sahara has been advancing into the Sahel, edge of the desert, thus threatening its small pastures. In Africa, where population is rapidly increasing, Animals kept for their meat and milk eat plants and destroy the soil preventing regrowth. Every year the desert increases by 15 million acres Africa is facing the threat of desertification.

Although the Sahara has popularity of being the largest desert, it is not true. The largest and the emptiest desert is the continent of Antarctica with an area of almost 5400000 sq mi (14000000 sq km) here water does not evaporate as on the Sahara but rather freezes. Thus, despite presence of water life cannot sustain. Plants cannot stick their roots into the ground. The continent if covered by a layer of ice 2.5 mi (4 km) thick. This ice never melts. All that melts is the peck ice with is the ice that covers the sea. When the temperature drops below freezing, the sea freezes over. The lowest recorded temperature is -126 F (-88C). Only penguins are the permanent residents of this desert. Yet it is the largest water reserve on the Earth. Its ice fields and icebergs make up 2/3 of fresh water in the world. Slowly flowing towards the sea, the glaciers break up and form icebergs- Mountains of unsalted ice. They float on the sea with only a 1/10 of their volume above the water, the rest lying beneath the surface. A few years ago, an American organization towed a huge iceberg to Saudi Arabia where is was used as a freshwater reserve. However, the experiment has not been repeated. This desert has the distinction of having the biggest glaciers on the Earth. The world's longest glacier is Lemert Glacier. Along with the adjoining Meller and Fisher Glaciers it extends for more than 300 mi (500 km)

Natural Bridges-Utah:

In Utah, if anywhere, the toil of man has made a reality of Biblical prophecy that the desert shell 'Rejoice and Blossom as rose'. It is a great natural wonderland also. There are three natural sandstone bridges among the largest examples of their kind. The largest is the rainbow natural bridge in the southeast. It is 300 ft above the bottom of the gorge, with a span of 278 ft. It is 56 ft thick at the top of the arc which is 37 ft wide. They show spectacular examples of the erosion caused by windblown sands. The two other bridges are slightly smaller. Nearer of the double arches is

200 ft high.

Carlsbad Caverns: New Mexico USA:

A cavern is an opening formed by natural action in a hill or mountain or beneath the earth's surface. Carlsbad Caverns are the largest in the world- regarded as the temple of the sun. They have been formed in limestone by water which trickles through the cracks and dissolves or wears away the stone. In these caverns strange formations were built up by calcium carbonate, dissolved by running water from the limestone of the caves. There are some pictures of animals and people on the walls. Cavemen of 3,500 years ago decorated these walls with crude drawings and outlines. They are sumptuously decorated with drip stone formation of both stalactites and stalagmites. There drapery conceal original limestone walls and the roof of the Queens chamber, a magnificent formation.

Luere caverns and Howe caverns also fall in this category. They attract many tourists. Outside the USA such caves exist in almost all parts of the world. They all present a marvelous site.

Crater Lake at Utah:

Just like an island sea a lake is an enclosed stretch of water. Crater Lake is a very deep body of water located in the crater of mount Mazama, an inactive volcano in the Cascade Mountains in the southwestern Oregon state of the US. It is one of the greatest scenic wonders of the world. Geologists believe the lake was formed thousands of years ago, after the glacial period when the top of Mount Mazama, then about 14,000 ft high, collapsed and was swallowed up outside the mountain. This left a huge saucer which was gradually filled by rain. This lake is dark blue in color, round and six miles across at the widest point. The surface is a little over 6,000 ft above sea level. The water us about 2,000 ft deep. There are no known outlets and streams flowing into this lake. A small volcano called Wizard Island was formed in the lake when later eruption of the lava came from the base of the mount Mazama. At first there were no fish in the Crater Lake, but trout were placed in the lake in 1888. Fish have been added each year. The Klamath Indians had legends about this mysterious lake. They believed that its waters had healing qualities. John Hillman, a mining prospector, discovered this lake in June 1853. He named it 'Deep Blue Lake'. The lake area was made a national park in 1902

The Great Barrier Reef:

The Great Barrier Reef is the largest coral formation in the world. Stretching for 2,000 km along Australia's northeast coastline, the reef is if the Great Wall of China, the greatest building project undertaken by mankind. The Great Wall is only 7.5 m high, but the Barrier Reef is an astounding 150 high. This is the largest single structure ever built by living creatures.

Part of the reef lies as near as 16 km to shore, while other parts are as far as 230 km from the coast, thus forming a wall between it and the open sea. This has been made up of a succession of reefs separated by channels. When storms are raging, the sharp reef blocks can be very dangerous to ships. The reef is helpful to sailors also. Once ships have passed it, they are shielded by storms of the open sea. It is a limestone formation which is produced by the activity of billions of tiny jelly like animals, known as Polyps, from two Greek words meaning 'Many feet'. The reef forming Polyps cannot live in waters colder than 65 F. This area near Australia has ideal temperature for their growth. The reef is the home of many other forms of life, such as brilliantly colored fishes, Star Fish, Mollusks and Sea Anemones.

When one dives near the reef one finds a multicolored world before him. Thousands of the variety of fish greet him. No one knows how long it took for this formation. Being a very slow process, it might have even taken millions of years. Now a days the reef is in danger. Since pearl and pearl shells are found in the water near the reef, a lot of human activity is present, damaging the formation. Some bring corals as souvenirs to decorate their drying rooms. The increasing shipping and consequent pollution of sea water is also causing havoc. World resources Institute has declared it an endangered formation. Increasing water temperature, due to warming of the earth, may reach the point that Algae living inside the Coral Polyps flee, leaving Corals without their main food source. Between natural and manmade stress, the barrier reef is now considered at risk.

CHAPTER SEVEN

Great Personalities: Pioneers of the World, Immortal Mortals

Moses: 1200 BC – 1080 BC:

A key figure in the Old Testament is the last prophet revered by the Jews, Christians and even the Muslims. After him there is no common prophet. He is the great leader of the early Hebrews who were one of the Semitic peoples. Their original home was in Arabia. They were attracted by the high civilization and good pastures for their flocks in Egypt. In the beginning, they were treated terribly. As their population increased, the Egyptians started treating them unkindly and forced them to lead a life of slavery.

When Moses was born, the Egyptian Pharaoh ordered that all Hebrew male children be killed because a prophecy had warned him that a child born on that day would destroy his kingdom. Afraid of the wrath of the Pharaoh, Moses' mother made a little boat of bulrushes and placed him in it among the reeds along the riverbank. One day the daughter of the Pharaoh came down to the river and found the boat with baby Moses inside. She felt sorry for the baby and decided to save his life by raising him as her own. Moses' mother became his nurse. After that he was brought up at Pharaoh's court. One day he saw an Egyptian beating an old Hebrew. He killed the Egyptian. He had to flee for his life. He went into Arabia to the distant land of Midian. There he cared for the flocks of a priest of Midianites, who was known as Jethro. Lately, Moses married his daughter. One day while minding the sheep in the desert he saw a bush that was on fire but remained unburned. He heard the voice of God saying upon him 'I have seen the misery of My people living in Egypt. Go. I send you before the Pharaoh to demand that my people, the children of Israel, leave Egypt to the promised land of Canaan, flowing with milk and honey that I promised to Abraham.'

So, Moses went to Egypt with his brother Aaron. When Pharaoh refused, ten great plagues came upon the country. The last plague killed all the first-born children of Egypt. The biblical story says that the houses of the Hebrew were spared by the Angel of Death. Then the pharaoh was obliged to let the Hebrew go. He changed his mind after the Hebrew left and chased them to the shores of the Red Sea. Moses then called to his people 'Fear not, the Lord shall fight for you'. A strong eastern wind divided the water and the Hebrew crossed over in safety. But when the Egyptians followed, the water rolled back. The entire army was destroyed.

Moses led his people across the Sinai desert- a journey that took them 40 years. When they arrived at the foot of Mount Sinai, Moses climbed the mountain to meet God, who had called him to the summit. While the people of Israel waited for Moses to come down the mountain, where he had remained for 40 days and 40 nights, they were terrified by the smoke and flames erupting from the top. The Ten Commandments engraved on two tablets that God gave to Moses on the mountain formed the fundamentals of the Jewish law providing a succinct summary of basic moralities and religious beliefs. Moses was not perfect. He became proud because he was the leader of the people. God told him he would never enter the promised land of Canaan. After several years he went to the top of another mountain, called Nebo, where he could see the land of Canaan. There, looking upon the land where his people were to live, he died at the age of 120. The Bible adds that no one knows where he is buried. The Jews look upon Moses as the founder of their nation, the organizer of their tradition, and the one who gave firm foundations to their religion.

Gautam Buddha: 600 BC:

Buddha is the title which was given to a young sage named Siddhartha who was the teacher, founder, and idol figure of the Buddhist religion, once prominent in Asia and half humans. Buddhists called him Gautam Buddha, which mean Fully Enlightened. He is still called Maser, Teacher and Divine Physician by people of the Buddhist faith.

He was born in 563 BC in Kapilvastu, Nepal as a prince. His father, Kind Shuddhi, had been informed by the priests that his son would become either a great emperor or a saint. The king tried bringing him up in an atmosphere of luxuries. He kept his son away from the shadow of sorrow. Once he came out of the palace and saw an old man Siddhartha felt sorry for him. Next time he saw a dead man being carried to the cremation grounds and followed by weeping relatives. He again felt sorry. Another day he saw a poor beggar in rags. He realized that there was too much sorrow in the world. Pity manifested in his heart and he felt a great desire to save people from sorrow.

One day Siddhartha gave up his palace, his inheritance and family in order that he might search for the truth to bring an end to the misery of mankind. He tried fasting and living as a hermit in the forest. After seven year of penance and wandering, he was sitting under a sacred fig tree when he realized the truth. He achieved enlightenment. This happened at Gaya, a town In Bihar (eastern India). Since then people called it Bodhgaya. Buddha believed that all sorrow of the world was caused by desire and selfishness. If one controls his desire, he will not be sorrowful. The way in which he planned that selfishness could be overcome formed the basis of the Buddhist religion.

After attaining enlightenment, he accepts pudding from Sujata, an untouchable woman. He declared that all human beings are equal: there is no difference between color, cast and status. All these features take mankind away from truth, satisfaction, and peace. He preached that sacred life is brotherly love. The woes of the world can be stamped out by a system known as 'The Eight-Fold Path'. These paths are right beliefs, right ideals, right words, right deeds, right meditation, right ways of living, right efforts, and right thinking. There are ten sins: three bodily (killing, theft and unchastity), four are sins of speech (lying, slander, abusive language, and useless conversation), three are of the mind (envy, malice, and disbelief). The secret of life is love of all creatures. Hatred never stops until it has come under the power of love. The well-trained mind holds a kindly attitude towards those around, above, and below him. Love of one's enemies is the crowning jewel of one's life. Nirvana (freedom from death and birth) can be attained by following the path. Nirvana is the goal of life.

After his preaching's, his religion was embraced by many people. Buddha achieved nirvana at the age of 80. In the third century BC, Ashoka the Great spread Buddhism throughout India and the neighboring countries. Even today there are about 200 million people in the world who follow his religion. Japan and the Southeast Asia are prominent.

Confucius: 551-479 BC:

Confucius became famous as a wise man: a sage of China. He said, 'what you do not like done to yourself, don't do unto others.' Several hundred years before Jesus, he pronounced this golden rule. Confucius was one of the most influential men who ever lived in China. The principals he taught are still the ideals of millions of people. The father of Confucius, a courageous soldier of royal descent, was the commander of a district in the state of Lu, China. He died when his son was three years old. The boy's mother had little money but gave him the best education available. At 15 years of age his mind was bent on learning. He mastered the teachings of the holy sages whose influence had made China a wise and united nation hundreds of years before his time. He decided that he must restore the faith and practices of the prophets, emperors, and sages of old.

Confucius was married when he was 19. By the time he was 21, he had a few students. He taught that the secret of good government was choosing honest and educated individuals. He was at one time appointed a high position in the government of Lu. His well governed district became a wonder of its time. Soon, however, he was compelled to resign because of a jealous duke. He travelled from place to place trying to find a prince who would listen to his teachings of just governments. He was misunderstood by most rulers of his time. Although he taught for 50 years, Confucius died practically unknown. Later the 'Five Classics' which record his wise teachings became the Confucius Bible. These books were used as textbooks in the Chinese schools. Even emperors considered Confucius 'Teacher of Teachers' and bowed at his shrines. He was contemporary to Buddha and Mahavir, the founder of Jainism. Confucianism is seen as a system of moral and philosophical teachings rather than a religion.

Jesus Christ:

Jesus Christ was the founder of the Christian religion. The Christians believe that he is the Son of God, who was sent to Earth to save Mankind. Scholars now believe that he was born in either 4 BC or 6 BC. No one is sure on what exact day of the year he was born. Since the 300's, December 25 has been celebrated as Christmas or his birthday. According to the New Testament Herod I, the king of Judaea, hearing that the wise men from the east were looking for the new king of Egypt, decided to kill the newborn to continue the reign of his heirs. He told three wise men that he needed to know the child's whereabouts, so that he could bow before him. The wise men found Jesus in a manger in Bethlehem and worshipped him by giving gifts of gold, incense, and myrrh. When the wise men did not return, Herod ordered his soldiers to kill every child less than two years old in Bethlehem. Warned by an angel of Herod's intentions, Mary and Joseph fled to Egypt with the child. After a few months Herod died. The couple then returned to Nazareth. Jesus grew to manhood here. Little is known about Jesus' life until he was 30. Probably he helped Joseph as a carpenter

At 30, Jesus knew he had come to fulfill a special mission in his life. His cousin, John the Baptist, (the voice of one crying out in the wilderness) had prepared the way for Him with His preaching's'. Jesus went to John to be baptized. John recognized him as the Messiah and told people who He was. Jesus then went into the wilderness to prepare for his mission. The devil tempted him to use his powers as the Son of God to become a great king and rule the world. Jesus Christ knew that he must live as a teacher for his people. When he came to the town, John the Baptist pointed him out to some of his followers at 'The Messiah'. These men became Jesus Christ's first disciples. The first four disciples were: Peter, Andrew, Jones, and John. Christ later picked eight more men to help him carry out his work. His first public appearance was at a wedding feast in Cana. Here he performed his first miracle: he turned water into wine when his host ran short. Jesus did not hesitate to tell people who he was. In Nazareth, he entered the Synagogue and announced that he was The Messiah. When he went to Jerusalem for the feast of Passover, he announced himself in the temple. The people in Jerusalem were impressed by many of the things he had to say. Then he left for Galilee which had been chosen as the place for his ministry to begin. His words spread rapidly among the people of Palestine. In the second year, he preached 'Sermon on the Mount' telling about his basic beliefs and teaching. It is also called the constitution of the kingdom of heaven. He gained many converts with the miracles he performed. He also gave to his disciples the power to perform miracles. They went about the land preaching his name.

Shortly before the end of the second year of his ministry, Jesus told his disciples that he must 'suffer many things and be killed'. He felt that if his teachings were to be fully understood and his ministry completed, he must die to save all men. On way to Jerusalem, many of the most important events in Jesus' career occurred. Among these were transfiguration, the healing of men born blind and the raising of Lazarus from the dead. Many Jews of Jerusalem were jealous of his popularity. On Sunday, he made a triumphant entry into the city. Thursday night he was with his disciples in Jerusalem, to celebrate he feast of Passover. This was The Last Supper, which is the source of Christian Eucharist.

Late on Thursday night he climbed the Mount Olives where he prayed. He was arrested by men sent by priests and Pharisees. He was tried before the Sanhedrin, the high Jewish court. He asked Jesus if he was the Son of God. Jesus Christ replied that he was. The found him guilty of blasphemy and sentenced him to death. He was made to carry a heavy wooden cross upon the road to the top of Mount Calvary. There was mailed to the cross. Before he died, he said 'Father, forgive them for they know not what they do'. He has influenced humanity more than anyone else who lived.

Prophet Mohammad:

Hazarat Mohammad, the founder of Islam, was born in 570 AD in Mecca, Saudi Arabia. His parents died when he was a child. He was brought up by his grandfather and uncle, Abu Talib. He used to go with his uncle on long journeys with the caravans to Arabia and Syria. Mohammad would often go to the town of the great city of Mecca, where large fares and religious meetings were held. There Heathens, Jews and Christians mingled and traded. There he heard talk of Pagan idols, God of Israel, and of Christ. At the age of 35 he entered the service of Khadijah, a wealthy woman. She was fifteen years older than him. He later married her. She had two sons and four daughters. The sons died while they were young. His daughter Fatima married Ali, the son of Abu Talim. They had two sons, Hassan, and Hussein, from whom many Muslims trace their descent back to Mohammad.

When Mohammad grew older, he often went out in the desert on a mountain side to think of God. One day he was meditating alone on Mount Hira when a vision suddenly appeared to him. In the vision the angel Gabriel told him to preach of God's nearness and to proclaim God's will to his people. At that time, he was 40. He went home and told his wife about his experience. He asked her if it could be possible that he was called to be a prophet of God. She said she knew from his goodness that the message must be true. With that she became his first disciple. After a while a rich merchant, Abu Bakr, and Omar, a town leader, became his disciples. A few poor people were converted. The majority, however, laughed at him. Some even stoned him from his teachings.

For 13 years Mohammad kept teaching patiently even while he was persecuted. In 619 AD, after the death of his wife and uncle, the hatred of the people of Mecca became very strong. In 622 he had to flee with his followers to Medina. This event is called "Hegira." The Muslim calendar starts from this date. In Medina people welcomed Mohammad and listened to him with great interest. His religion spread rapidly. The people of Medina made him their King. The people of Mecca attacked Medina again and again. Mecca was finally defeated. Mohammad then entered his native city under a triumphal procession.

Many of the Arab tribes accepted hi religion. Before he died, he was the prophet-leader of the greater part of Arabia. As leader, Mohammad did away with old customs of worshipping idols and killing baby girls at birth. He limited the practice of Polygamy and divorce. He reformed laws of inheritance, regulated slavery and gave aid to poor. He approved war and conquest yet was tolerant of Jews and Christians if they surrendered. He founded a new religion and a new state on the unity of God and the brotherhood of man.

Saint Peter the First Pope:

Jesus entrusted St. Peter to establish the Christian Church, and he's regarded as the first Pope, or head of the Church. To spread the teachings of Christ, St. Peter traveled to many parts of the Roman Empire, settling in Rome. He had established a church in Jerusalem, on the first Pentecost after the resurrection and ascension of Christ (about 30 A.D.). Jesus singled out Peter on several occasions for special consideration. He sat in Peter's boat to preach to the multitude on the shores of Lake Gennesaret. When Jesus was walking on the water of the lake, He called to Peter to come to him across the lake. He chose Peter to stay with him in the garden of Gethsemane, the night before the crucifixion. The angel who appeared before the women at Christ's tomb on the morning of Resurrection gave a special message. Christ chose Peter of all the Apostles as the one to whom he appeared to on the day of Resurrection. Later he gave him special orders to spread the faith at a meeting with the Apostles.

After the Ascension, Peter began his mission in which he did not falter until his death. In A.D. 42 King Herod had him thrown into prison to be executed. Peter escaped through a miracle and left Palestine. He traveled widely in the near East. His first Epistle was addressed to the Christians of Pontus, Galatia, Cappadocia, and Asia. At some time, he came to Rome and preached there for several years. Along with St. Paul he founded the Roman Catholic Church. He may have been killed during the persecutions of the emperor Nero.

The Romans had not tolerated Christ, nor did they tolerate St. Peter. Peter was crucified between A.D 64 and A.D. 68. His successors stayed in Rome. In 1506, the largest Christian Church in the world was built over the tomb or crypt containing the tomb of St. Peter. The crypt is part of an early church built by Constantine the Great between 323 and 326 A.D. According to legends, many early Christian martyrs were put to death there. Only the Pope or an authorized cardinal may hold service there. St. Peter's Church can hold about 35,000 persons. Canonization is celebrated only in

St. Peter's Church.

Hammurabi:

About 2000 B.C, Hammurabi ruled Babylonia for about43 years as the sixth king of the first dynasty. He did much to strengthen his kingdom by conquest, but his greatness lay in his capability as an administrator. His reign is known as the "Golden Age of Babylonia," a region between the Tigris and Euphrates Rivers in modern Iraq. It is regarded as the cradle of the civilization of Sumer, Akkad, Babylonia, and Assyria. Hammurabi, at the time of colonization in 1792 B.C, was confronted by numerous small neighboring kingdoms. All wanted to dominate Babylonia. In a series of battles, he defeated the kingdoms of Lars, Mari, and Assyria. Hammurabi was an Amorite (the previous king had been Sumerians).

After consolidating his position, he devoted himself to the welfare of his people. He built irrigation canals to improve agriculture. He set up systems of maximum prices and minimum wages and reorganized taxation on a fair and efficient bases. He also made the Acadian language, spoken by the common people, the official language. The great code of law by Hammurabi was written in Acadian.

He is famous for the codification of the laws for the first time in the world. His code was the collection of Babylonian laws which he had organized systematically. The code was engraved on a stele (column) of Basalt (a hard, black stone) which was discovered at Susa in southwest of Iran in 1901 A.D. It had been carried off as booty by an Elamite king. On the top of the Code, Hammurabi, king of Babylon, is standing before the sun god Shamash who is ordering him to establish just and righteous laws. Therefore, Hammurabi always referred to himself as "He Who Established Justice on Earth". The gist of law was "an eye for an eye and a tooth for a tooth." The code greatly influenced the civilization of all near Eastern countries. It had almost 300 legal provisions. The laws covered false accusation, witchcraft, military service, land and business laws, family rights, tariffs, wages, trades, loans, and debts. The tone of the code was that "the strong shall not injure the weak." It set up a social order based on the rights of the individual protected by the authority of law. Hammurabi is also known for the correspondence he conducted with his neighbors- before proceeding to dominate them.

Wise King Solomon:

Solomon, the most famous king as described in the Old Testament, was the son of David and succeeded him as the king of Israel, from around 970 B.C. to 971 B.C. When David was on his death bed, Solomon's mother Bathsheba and others of the court successfully plotted to give him the throne. He added much to the wealth David had left. He brought fine horses from other lands into his country and sold them for high prices. He also built up a fleet of trading vessels that sailed from the head of the Gulf of Aqaba down the Red Sea to the land of Ophir. He also traded with Southern Arabia. In the Land of Eden, Solomon mined rich copper and iron which were carried down the valley and smelted at Aqaba. It is a small wonder that the Biblical historian exclaimed "So King Solomon exceeded all the kings of the earth in riches". He received Queen of Sheba at his palace in Jerusalem. She gave him gifts of rare species, precious stones and 120 talents of gold worth, about $3,490,200.

He transformed Jerusalem from a lowly city into a great capital. These were peaceful times. There were advancements in art and literature. He put to good use the wealth that was gained in trade. The most famous building built by him was the Temple. Nothing now remains of that Temple, except the Western Wall or Wailing Wall. This is a place of Jewish pilgrimage. According to the Bible, this temple stood on the spot where Abraham prepared to sacrifice Isaac. Erected between 966 and 959 B.C., it housed the Arc of the Covenant, the chest containing the stone tablets engraved with the Ten Commandments given by God to Moses. Solomon's own palace was the largest and the most gorgeous.

The Bible tells how Solomon was known throughout the eastern world as a wise man. Many fables are told about the Wisdom of Solomon. He assembled at his court a group of the finest scholars and writers of the time. He himself took part in the discussions of the learned men at the court. It is said that he wrote the Book of Proverbs, the "Song of Solomon". The Jewish and Christian religions think the song is a story, which teaches or explains something else. The Jews think, it pictures the close connection between God and Israel. The Christians think it suggests the union of the Christ and the Church. However, all agree that Solomon was one of the wisest and noblest kings of all times.

Nebuchadnezzar II:

Nebuchadnezzar II was a king told about in the Old Testament. He ruled Babylonia from 605 -562 B.C. Like Hammurabi one thousand years before him, he was the most powerful king of that time. He captured Jerusalem in 586 BC and destroyed the city. This battle was the end of Hebrew kingdom and the beginning of the "Babylonian Captivity". The Old Testament also tells of his spells of madness, when he would imagine himself as an ox and would go out in the field to eat grass.

Nebuchadnezzar was the son of Nabopolassar, the founder of the Chaldean or new Babylonian empire. Under his rule Babylon became of the most magnificent cities of the ancient world. In his own records, he rarely mentioned his military activities, but wrote of his various building activities and his attention to the many Gods of Babylonia. He built the 'Hanging Gardens', one of the seven wonders of the ancient world. He did this to please his beloved wife who was a princess from the Median Hills and missed the greenery and flowers of her native lands. He made artificial hills and indigenous systems to irrigate on the heights. He was at war with Phoenician City of Tyre and attacked the city unsuccessfully for 13 years. He also fought an indecisive campaign against Egypt in the last part of his reign. Thus he was both a warrior and administrator. With its grandiose royal building Babylon became the political capital and religious center of the empire. Although pillaged and destroyed by the Hittites and by Elamites, the city was always re-born. The administrative structures perfected by Nebuchadnezzar are known to the world thanks to the extensive records that survive on clay tablets written by the Scribes.

Cyrus the Great:

Cyrus the Great (600-529 BC), sometimes call Cyrus the Elder, founded the ancient Persian empire. His ancestors have been vassals of Median King ruling over Anshan near the Persian Gulf. There is a legend that Cyrus' Grandfather Astyages tried to have him killed when he was an infant. Astyages was warned by Soothsayers, that he might be overthrown by his grandson. Cyrus was protected by a shepherd and was eventually restored to his parents. When he grew up, he began his remarkable career by collecting a vast army of Persians, with which he overthrew his Grandfather and became the king of Media and Persia. He next made himself master of Lydia, by defeating Croesus, in 546 BC. A few years later, he defeated Nabonidus, King of Babylon. Cyrus was a wise, generous ruler. He permitted the Jews to return to Jerusalem from captivity in Babylonia. He took the title "King of the World" and spent 10 years organizing his kingdom. Although he had added all Asia Minor to Persia, he still wanted more Lands. While conducting an expedition against, Scythians, he was slain. The Tomb of Cyrus the Great was made at Pasargadae, in modern Iran. His body laid here from the time of his death in battle in 529 BC, until the arrival of Alexander the Great in 330 BC.

Ashoka the Great:

Ashoka was the greatest emperor of India in the pre-Christ era. He was the grandson of Chandragupta Maurya, who founded the first dynasty, in 321 BC in Magadh, only 5 years after the invasion of Alexander. Chandragupta was succeeded by his son Bindusara, the father of Ashok. In 273 BC, Ashok succeeded him. The first four years were spent in consolidating his position. During his period he destroyed his adversaries and other Clements. After this he paid attention to other kingdoms, which were trying to take advantage of confusing situation in Magadh. Soon several wars were fought and by 269 BC the whole of India, expect Kalinga (modern Orissa), was under his rule. He was crowned in 269BC. He was a brave and ambitious ruler, with a benevolent attitude towards people in general. In 261 BC, he attacked Kalinga, the last resort of independent rulers. It was the fiercest war; Ashok had ever fought. One hundred thousand people were killed and one hundred and fifty thousand injured badly. Not a single male fighter survived in Kalinga. At last the princess came with an army of women to fight. Ashoka was stunned to see this scene. The large-scale massacre filled him with remorse, and he took a vow, not to fight for territory anymore. Rather he would win the territories by winning the hearts of people.

He became a Buddhist and renounced the war forever. Now the public welfare was his only priority. He got built roads, wells, shelters, orphanages and prohibited hunting by law. it was time of great peace. He got engrave Buddha's teachings on pillars and rocks. His kingdom included, whole of India, Afghanistan, and part of modern Iran. Being a great proponent of Buddhism, he travelled to all the places, of Buddhist pilgrimage and got built so many 'Viharas' (residential buildings for Buddhist monks), in the Magadh, that the whole area came to be known as 'Bihar' (Modern India State).

In his time, Buddhism became state religion and well-organized institution (Sangh). Ashoka wanted to spread this peaceful religion to the other parts of the world also. Therefore he sent thousands of Buddhist priests to the neighboring countries such as Afghanistan, Iran, Sri Lanka, Tibet, China, and South East Asia. To pursue the cause of world peace with vigor and enthusiasm, he prepared his own children to take up the cause. His son, Mahindra, and daughter Sanghmitra, renounced the comforts of the palace and became 'Bhikkhus' (priests). They went to the neighboring countries, to spend the light of the Buddha. India's two most prominent International Universities, Nalanda and Takshila, got a big boost during his times. By the time Ashoka dies in 236 BC, his empire was a great island of peace in the vast ocean of turmoil.

Harun Al Rashid:

Harun Al Rashid was one of the most famous Caliphs of the Islamic world. Caliph is the tile of the rulers, who succeeded Prophet Mohammed, both as spiritual and civil leaders. The office of a Caliph and dominion ruled by him are called a 'Caliphate'. After the Prophet died, his followers wanted to establish an empire, where all who believed in Islam, would be under one supreme ruler or Caliph. Between 632 and 750 AD, Caliphs were recognized by all Muslims. But in 750 AD, Islam became divided. Thereafter several rival hereditary Caliphates were established in various parts of the world. But the Caliphate of Baghdad had long been established before 750 AD and was respected by all the Muslims of the world. Harun Al Rashid (764 – 809 AD), was the 5th ruler of this Caliphate. He became Caliph, or head of the Muslims, in 786 AD and quickly suppressed all rebellions. He was very popular ruler and highly devoted to public welfare.

He used to walk around the town of Baghdad and other areas in disguise at night to get the firsthand knowledge of the state affairs and his subjects. Sometimes, he did not return to the capital for days. Therefore he gave control of state affairs to his grand Wazir 'Yahiya'. Harun Al Rashidloved luxury and pleasure and was a great patron of learning, music and art. Baghdad became the resort of most prominent Muslims of the times. It is said that in 4 years, 100,000 workers, directed by great Arab architects, built a beautiful city on the banks of the River Tigris, though little of it now remains. The most famous storybook in the world "the Arabian Nights" was written on the inspiration of the Caliph Harun Al Rashid. In this storybook, his Queen "Scheherazade", relates the life of the Caliph of Bagdad, weaving into this account the legends and tales that her master loved. These were told in an unbroken chain in 1001 nights. They include 'Aladdin and the Magic Lamp', 'Alibaba and the 40 Thieves', 'Voyages of Sinbad', 'Love story of Laila and Majnu' etc.

Homer:

Homer is the oldest name in European literary history. The Greek poet is one of the greatest figures in all literature as the writer of 'Iliad' and 'Odyssey'. Some scholars have even questioned whether he really lived. They have said that the poems called Homers' were just a collection of poems by many people, lumped together under his name. Now it is generally agreed that he was a real person who wrote the poems called 'His'. There is no Unanimity about his times; it varied from 1100 BC to 600 BC in different accounts. Now it is generally believed that he lived during the 800 BCs and was born in Asia Minor, not far from Troy (now in Turkey). Seven cities claim to be his birthplace. The Greeks loved his works and made him the center of their literary education. It is still debated whether all 27,800 verses of the 'Iliad' and 'Odyssey' were indeed composed by him. Greeks told many stories about him, but it seems certain that he was blind and very poor. He wandered from town to town telling his stories to the music of a lyre. His work was a culmination of a long oral tradition told from 10 century BC, when bards travelled to courts to sing the exploits of legendary heroes.

It is known that Homer's poems were recited in the Greek state of Sparta around 500 BC. Each Greek city state had its own treasured copies of the poems. It is said that Alexander the Great slept with a copy of the epics at his head, as he considered them to be the best war manuals. During the Dark Ages, Europeans lost the knowledge of his Classics. Peoples of the Middle East kept them alive. A renewed interest in the poems was a major force in the intellectual awakening of the Renaissance.

Homer's poems were hailed as the greatest poetical masterpieces of all time. His works were set up as the standard towards which all poets showed strive. The reading of 'Iliad' and 'Odyssey' came to be one of the major parts of school courses. In 'Iliad' much of the action centers around the exploits of the Greek Achilles, who during the siege of troy withdrew to his tent and refused to fight. Achilles' anger is due to the Greek commander, Agamemnon, having abducted Briseis, a prisoner of war with whom Achilles was in love. Unlike 'Iliad', the 'Odyssey' was the story of one man, Ulysses, whose weaknesses is matched by his resourcefulness. However, his escape from the dangers he encounters, is due to the intervention of gods on his behalf. It is an adventure story told in verse. These two poems represented an important advance in western culture. They were one of the first stories told about God and Man. We have much knowledge about the olden times from Homer's works.

Socrates:

Socrates (469-399 BC) was one of the greatest Greek philosophers. He left no writings of his philosophies. They are known through his student Plato's writings. His guiding principle was 'Know thy Self'. He believed that goodness was based on knowledge and wickedness was based on ignorance. He argued that no man is bad. He sought truth all his life. His chief work was among the young men of Athens. He thought it was his duty to lead them to a nobler, moral life. His method of instruction is known as Socratic Method. It was a cross examination which tangled even the wisest in a net of errors. He would pretend to know nothing of the subject under discussion. By a series of carefully directed questions he would make the other person find out the truth for himself.

He was born in Athens as the son of a sculpture. He received little education in his youth later became familiar with the best philosophy and thought of his time. He walked in the street and marketplaces talking to people about the soul and moral life of man in general. He was not popular as a teacher. He had an ugly appearance. His body was short and squat. His walk was like a Pelican's waddle. He was too taken up with his work to worry about his looks. His wife, Xanthippe, was a bad-tempered woman. He lived with her to teach himself self-control. He was also a noted solider. He fought in Delium and Amphipolis in 424 BC. He gained a wide reputation for his bravery. However he refused to take part in public affairs, as he was afraid, he would have to go against his senses of truth and justice is he participated. After the naval battle of Arginase in 406 BC, he spoke against the citizens when they unjustly demanded the death of 10 generals who had been unable to bury the dead. Again in 404 BC, during the period of terror which followed the death of Pericles, Socrates went against the orders of the Trinity Tyrants who ruled Athens. He would have been condemned to death for it had the government of the Trinity Tyrants not been overthrown.

His unflinching honesty and habit of probing and ironic questioning earned him the enmity of the Athenian authorities. In 399 BC he was charged with introducing new Gods and not worshipping the old ones. He was also charged with corrupting the youth of Athens by his teaching. He refused to have a lawyer. Instead he gave his own defense, the famous 'Apology of Socrates', which explained his life. He proved that he was not being tried for any crime. His beliefs and way of life were a menace to the tyranny of the state. He was found guilty and condemned to death. His death was both dramatic and heroic. He serenely drank a cup of Hemlock poison which was handed to him and died in conversation with his students.

William Shakespeare:

William Shakespeare is the greatest name not only in English Literature but in World Literature. Born in 1564 AD, he is usually considered the greatest dramatist and finest poet the world has known. No other writer's plays have been produced so many times in so many countries in so many languages. No poet's verse has been so widely read in so many different lands. His works have been translated into more languages than any book in the world except for the Bible. Thousands upon Thousands of books and articles have been written upon him and his works.

He was born in Stratford-on-Avon, an important English market town about 80 miles northwest of London into a family of glove makers and wood traders. Not much is known of his early life. It is certain though that in 1592 he was recognized and an actor and a playwright in London. When the theater was closed due to plague and riots, he wrote 'Venus and Adonis' and the 'The Rape of Lucrecia'. Both became very popular. They added to his growing reputation. His fortune was pegged with theater. He joined the 'Lord Chamberlin's Company' and became partner in the Globe Theater and Black Fryer's Theater. He was a professional dramatist and wrote his plays to sooth the taste of the theater audience. In general, his plays fall into three classes: comedies, histories, and tragedies. His comedies show greater variety than either of his histories or tragedies. The most famous are: As you like it, Twelfth night and a Midsummer night's Dream. The Comedy of Errors and Taming of the Shrews are light romances with an aim to satisfy the demand of London audience for stories about the past. He wrote about 10 histories, of his Richard the Second, Henry 4, Henry 6, Henry 6, Edward 4, Edward 5, and Richard 3, became quite popular. His real genius flowered in his tragedies: Macbeth, Othello, King Lear, and Romeo Juliet. People feel touched after reading them.

One of the reasons for Shakespeare's worldwide appeal is the number and variety of characters he created. They include people of all type, from all walks of life. He understood his characters so deeply and presented him so vividly that they have become more real than the people they represent. This is especially true about Shylock, Falstaff, Macbeth, Hamlet, Rosalyn, Richard 2, Beatrice, Brutus, King Lear, Marc Anthony, and Iago.

He died at the age of 52 on April 23, 1616. As a prominent citizen of the town he was buried inside the Chancel of Holy Trinity Church. All his 37 plays and poems have universal appeal, which has made him the greatest man of literature and darling of the people for all time.

CHAPTER EIGHT

Great Personalities: Conquerors'

Alexander the Great:

Phillip 2, king of Macedonia, extended his power of all of Greece by exercising political skill as well as military means. In 336 BC, when he was planning a war against the Persians, he was murdered. He was succeeded by Alexander at age 20, who was already well prepared in the art of government and war under the guidance of Aristotle. Adopting the slogan of a Hellenic crusade against the barbarians, he occupied Syria- and after a long siege of Tyre-Phoenicia he entered Egypt, where he was accepted as Pharaoh.After organizing Egypt and founding Alexandria, he crossed the eastern desert and the Euphrates and Tigris rivers. In the autumn of 331 BC, he defeated Darius 3 at Gaugamela (near modern Irbil, Iraq), causing the great Persian empire to tumble down. Alexander occupied the imperial capital Susa and Persepolis. Henceforth he acted as the legitimate emperor of the Persian Empire.

His preoccupation in the east inspired some of the nobles in Greece to raise a banner of revolt. Unfortunately it was crushed. With discipline restored, Alexander invaded India (327 BC). He conquered most of Punjab. He was stopped from pressing on to the distant Ganges by a mutiny of soldiers who were scared by the powerful army of Magadh Empire. Turning south, he marched down to the mouth of the Indus. There he engaged in some of the heaviest fighting and heaviest massacres of the war. With no morale and a tired army, he was compelled to return. In the spring of 324 BC he held a great victory celebration at Susa where weak soldiers and nobles married Iranian women. He gave them rich wedding gifts. His aim was apparently to prepare a long-term solution by breeding a new body of high nobles with mixed blood. He was preparing for a conquest of Arabia when he fell ill with malaria. He died in June 323 without designating a successor.

His historical legacy was the spread of a veneer of Greek culture far into central Asia: the acceptance of the idea of a universal kingdom which prepared the way for the Roman Empire. It also opened the Greek World to new oriental influence, which prepares the way for Christianity. Alexander's invasion shook the world and brought it closer.

Hannibal: 247-143 BC:

He was the greatest general and statement of Ancient Carthage. His masterly strategy and his talent for overcoming handicaps ranked him very high with the military genius of ancient times. His skill enabled him to defeat enemies who had much larger armies than he had. He promised his father, Hamilcar Barca, to carry on the fighting against the Romans who had tried to bring North Africa under their power. From Carthage he was taken to Spain and trained for a military career when he was still a boy. At the age of 25, he became commander of the army in Spain. Hannibal believed that the Roman's should be conquered in Italy, so he made careful plans to attack them there, at heart. He marched across the Pyrenees Mountains, the Rhone River, and on into Italy.

He brought elephants with him from Africa to break the ranks of Roman legionaries. This long trail across the mountains and rivers cost him many men and most of his elephants. The mountain paths were very narrow and steep. The elephants often lost their balance and fell over cliffs to their death. Hannibal's army of 20,000 infantry men and 6,000 horsemen seemed only a handful compared to the army of 700,000 Roman men. He reached the Rhone River before the Romans could stop him. He defeated the army under the command of Scipio on the bank of Ticinus River.

Immediately after this battle he met and defeated two armies at once at the Trebbia River in 218 BC. Next year he defeated the Roman general Flaminius and marched into Apulia. In 216 BC the battle of Cannae ended in the defeat for the Romans and cost them 50,000 men.

He set up his headquarters in Capua to give him troops rest after several battles. He thought at this point that Rome would collapse. He was mistaken. The Romans used two field armies to make minor nuisance raids without risking a major battle. These tactics wore down Hannibal's forces. In 207 BC, Roman's wiped out an army led from Spain led by his brother Hasdrubal and drove the Carthaginians out of Spain. Scipio carried the war into Africa to release the pressure of Hannibal on the Romans in Europe. In 203 BC Hannibal was called home to defend his country against Scipio. He was defeated at Zama in 202 BC, after 18 years of warfare.

Carthage was forced to accept the most shameful terms of peace. Hannibal was no longer a general in the army. He became the leader in civic life of Carthage and tried to restore its prosperity. He was so successful that jealous Romans sent ambassadors to Carthage to oust Hannibal. He fled to Ephesus and offered to help Antiochus 3 of Syria in his war against the Romans, which had just started. He was put in charge of the Syrian fleet but was defeated and had to flee to Crete. At last he found safety in Bithynia. Hannibal had been there only for a short time when the Romans sent Flaminius to demand his surrender. Hannibal preferred death to becoming a prisoner of the Romans. He took poison, which he had hidden in a secret hiding place in his fingernail. He was the greatest general who dared Romans in their homeland and defeated them several times.

Julius Caesar:

Julius Caesar (100-44 B.C.), Roman general and statesman was one of the greatest man in history. He was born in Rome in an aristocratic family, but his sympathies were with the People's Party. He believed firmly that the people in provinces should have the rights of Roman citizens and favored doing away with aristocratic privileges. At the age of 17, he married Cornelia, the daughter of Luscious Cornelius Cinna, the leader of the People's Party. He refused to divorce her at the command of the aristocrats. He was forced to leave Rome and give up all his property. After the death of Sulla, the dictator of Rome, he returned. He was sent to Spain as the governor where he stayed for a year. In 60 B.C. he and two other leaders formed an alliance to rule Rome. They were Marcus Licinius, a wealthy man, and Gnaesus Pompey, a great military leader. Caesar was elected consul in 59 B.C.

He went to Gaul (France) and in his 9 campaigns there he brought the whole province under his control by driving Germans out. This brought him immense popularity in Rome where a public Thanksgiving function was held in his honor. He invaded Britain twice in 55 and 554 B.C. Now Pompey began to oppose him and became alarmed at his success. In 49 B.C., Pompey persuaded the Senate to order Caesar's army broken. Caesar did not oblige. This was the beginning of the civil war. There was little bloodshed in Caesar's march on Rome and within 60 days, he had made himself master of all Italy. In 49 B.C. he was appointed dictator and consul as well as tribune for life. Caesar followed Pompey to Greece and defeated him in 48 B.C. He followed him to Egypt and found that Pompey had been murdered.

Before returning to Rome, Caesar was also victorious in the war which he fought to place Cleopatra, his beloved, on the throne of Egypt. He later brought to Rome. His victories included one over Pharnaces II, king of Pontus, in 47 B.C. in West Asia and at Thapsus, in Northern Africa in 46 B.C. Caesar fought his last battle in 45 B.C. at Munda, Spain. There he defeated two sons of Pompey. He was now the undisputed master of the Roman world and pardoned the followers of Pompey. People honored him for his leadership and triumphs by granting the powers of a dictator for 10 years. He was, then, made dictator for life and his portrait was stamped upon Roman coins. At a public festival the people, represented by Mark Antony, offered him the crown but he refused. Still, the aristocrats suspected that he wanted to make himself king. His fast friend, Marcus Junus Brutus, and Ganius Cassius led the aristocrats in a plot to kill Caesar. On March 15th, 44 B.C. Caesar was stabbed to death as he entered a Senate meeting. He received more than 20 wombs from the daggers of the man who had accepted his favors and who he had believed were his friends.

Caesar used the powers he had won to good advantage and made many important reforms. He improved the calendar and cleared up confusion that had existed in computing time for 100 years. He appointed the most capable persons to the public offices. He granted Roman citizenship to many of the people in the provinces. He encouraged poor people in Rome to establish colonies in Carthage and Corinth. He was a great auditor and writer too. He ranks very high among conquerors and reformers.

After his death, the Roman Republic ended, and his nephew Octavian became the emperor with the title of Augustus Caesar. All Roman emperors adopted the title of "Caesar." Such was his impact on history.

Attila the Hun:

Hun was a wondering and warlike Mongolian tribe. In the 5th century, they became very powerful under their leader Attila, who harassed the eastern half of the Roman Empire during the 440s and devastated much of the western half of the empire in 451-52 A.D. Before that the Hun had moved westward across the Volga River, about 350 A.D. and defeated the Alani, another tribe of barbarians. Then they conquered and drove out the Goats. Under Attila they became very powerful. Attila was born near the river Danube in 395 A.D. He had completed his education at the court of Emperor Honorius in Rome where he developed a hatred for the Romans.

In 434 A.D., Attila, and his brother Bleda negotiated a treaty with the Eastern Roman (Byzantine) –emperor Theodosius II and obtained an immense annual tribute of about 300 kg of gold. After 6 years of peace, the Huns invaded the empire and defeated several imperial armies. After another treaty and payment of more tribute, peace was made. In 445 A.D., Attila murdered his brother and launched a new campaign. He struck again in 440 and forced the emperor to cede large areas south of the Danube to the Huns. He later attacked Romans in Gaul (France) and in Italy, terrorizing the population. According to legend, wherever Attila passed with his hordes of horseman, the grass never grew again. In 450, he again attacked Gaul. A coalition of imperial forces, Visigoths, and other peoples especially Alans, was formed by the Roman General Aetius. Attila's goal was stopped at Orleans and he was forced to retreat. In 451, at the battle of Catalaunum plains (near Chalons) Aetius' forces one a decisive victory and Attila retreated. In 452 A.D. he attacked Italy but was turned back by an epidemic. He died in 453 A.D. Because of the cruelties he perpetrated and these exploits, he came to be known as the "Scourge of God."

Genghis Khan:

In medieval time, Mongolia was populated by Nomads, led by chiefs called Khans. These nomads believed that their mission was to dominate and pacify all the people of the world. In 1206 A.D., on chief, Temujin, assumed the title of Genghis Khan (Universal Ruler). He was only 13 when he succeeded his father as the chief of the tribe. He soon proved that he was a military genius. He subdued revolts among the Tatars and became the ruler of United Mongol and Tatar Tribes. He claimed that he had a divine call and so inspired his soldiers that they willingly followed him to battle. He set about conquering his neighbors. The Chin Empire in northern China crumpled in 1215 A.D. when he captured Beijing. He then proceeded to destroy Bukhara and Samarkand, while another of his armies reached Kiev.

His hordes, fearsome horsemen from Mongolia conquered Afghanistan and western Iran. They entered India but Sultan Iltutmish persuaded them to return by giving them a lot of gold. Notorious for killing, looting, and burning, they spread terror in their path. In 1225, Genghis Khan and kingdom of Tangut (Southwestern China), Now Genghis Khan was the ruler of a vast empire which included Manchuria, Mongolia, most of China, Turkestan, Afghanistan, northern Iran, Siberia, and most of Russia. The lands conquered by Genghis Khan marked his as one of the greatest military leaders in history. Genghis Khan tried to bring a lot of changed among the Mongols. He got their first written code of law, the Yassa, published in 1219. Its outlawed murder, looting, and other kinds of violence as well as adultery and drunkenness. The power of the Mongols stemmed above all from their military organization and discipline. His sons and grandsons spread the empire too far off places.

When Genghis Khan died in 1277 after leading the Mongols for 71 years, his empire stretched from the north of China to the Caucasus Mountains in Georgia. His grandson Kublai Khan, whom Marco Polo met, carried the legacy of Genghis Khan in China.

Western Europe was threatened by Batu, one of Khan's grandson's, who turned back from the gates of Vienna and he heard that his father had died. The Mongols established the biggest empire in the world that stretched from China to almost whole of Europe and Russia in north to Afghanistan in the south. This empire lasted for almost 100 years and brought the world closer.

Napoleon Bonaparte:

After Alexander the Great and Genghis Khan, Napoleon was the most dominating personality and great military genius of the world. His violent career changed the face of Europe. He overcame army after army until it seemed as if he could not be defeated. Almost whole of Europe was at war with him for 20 years. Despite somewhat disappointing appearance he had a remarkable career. His mother encouraged and aided him in his rise from moderate circumstances to the height of power. His soldiers adored him. He could personally direct complicated military maneuvers and at the same time control the press, the detailed police system, the intricate foreign policy, and the home government. But his personal life was unhappy and unsuccessful. Finally he brought about his own downfall.

He was born at Ajaccio in Corsica on August 15, 1769 A.D. He entered the military school at the age of 10. Although, not brilliant with studies, it was noticed that he had confidence in his own judgment and persistence in carrying out decisions. These qualities later made him feared equally in the Counsel Chamber and on the battlefield. He received his commission in artillery in 1785. During the French Revolution he took part in the occupation of Marseilles by the revolutionary forces. He earned generalship in the army when he was only 24. After the fall of Robespierre in 1794, he fell on bad days. The Convention which then governed France was becoming very unpopular. At that time, on the invitation of Paul Barras, the commander in chief of the Convention forces, he cleared the streets of Paris from the Royalists.

At this time Napoleon grabbed power. The "whiff of grapeshot," from his gun the day he cleared the streets of Paris made October 5, 1795 a red lettered day in Europe. In the meantime, he married Josephine, who was 16 years older and who never remained faithful to him. After the Italian campaign in 1797, Napoleon became a national hero. At home, under a conspiracy to keep him away, he was sent to Egypt to quell the British power. When he was fighting in Egypt, he learned about the conspiracy against him at Paris. Leaving the command of the army to General Jean Cleber, he arrived suddenly in Paris and by a bold stroke known as the "Coup d'état" of 18th Brumaire, abolished the power of ruling Junta, the directory. The little corporal from Corsica had become the ruler of France. Under his supervision, the laws of France were codified and redrawn. In 1800 A.D., he established the Bank of France. Finding France in dire straits, he arranged the sale of Louisiana Territory covering nearly 1million square miles to the USA for $15,000,000.

He had a dream for an eastern empire by conquering Egypt and then marching onto India. But the supremacy of the British navy compelled him to abandon it and he turned his attention to Europe. On December 2nd, 1800 he defeated Austria. Now Britain remained as France's active enemy. Spain, Naples, Bavaria, Portugal, Russia, Turkey, and even Britain had all been forced to make treaties with Napoleon. In May 1804, the French Senate offered him the title of "emperor" and on December 4, 1804 he was crowned as the emperor Napoleon I at Notre Dame Cathedral in the presence of Pope Pius VII. By 1805, the continent was under his hegemony. In 1806, Prussia was defeated. He inflicted a crushing defeat on Russia in 1807. The Treaties of Tilsit were signed. The same year he occupied Portugal.

Josephine could not give him an heir, so he divorced her and married Archduchess Mary Louise of Austria. Russia had not been able to carry out fully the provisions of the treaty, so he marched eastward. This was a blunder. The Russians allowed him deeper. Winter came and his army was marooned and destroyed in the snow. He hastened back to Paris but in March 1814 powers aligned against him. Napoleon accepted defeat and was exiled at the island of Elba. He escaped and on March 1, 1815 he landed in the south of France, raised an army, and marched on Paris. The four great powers- Britain, Austria, Prussia, and Russia- renewed their alliance against him. A battle finally took place at Waterloo near Brussels on June 18, 1815. Despite the great courage shown by the French, his army was defeated. He was exiled to St. Helena of the west coast of Africa where he died of cancer on 5th May 1821. Thus ends, the saga of a great general. His mortal remains lay under the golden dome of the Cathedral of Notre Dame.

Adolf Hitler:

Adolf Hitler was the most controversial leader of all time. He is the most maligned, hated and yet most admired for his leadership and oratory. He is the Saturn of Milton and Fallen Hero of the 20th Century. So long as there is history of war Hitler will remain immortal. 'Conquest', Hitler told the German people, 'Is not only a right but also a duty with us as we the superior Aryans have been chosen by God to rule the world.' He was dictator of Germany for 12 eventful years. With fanatical faith in his own mission, he united the German people through his doctrine of extreme nationalism. He had such wholehearted support from the Germans that they followed his leadership even though the path led to World War.

The Fuehrer, as Hitler called himself, was the first ruler of Germany who rose from the common mass. He was born in 1889 in the Austrian town of Braunau on the Inn. In his early life he studied art, music, and architecture. After his mother's death in 1908 he led five miserable years. He refused to become a civil servant. At that time he was sickly, lazy, dirty, and often hungry. 'The outbreak of World War 1', Hitler later said, 'brought salvation from the rotten experiences from my youth'. In August 1914 he enlisted in the Bavarian army. He never rose above the rank of Lance Corporal. The fact that he failed to become an officer filled him with resentment, strongly influencing his character. After the war in 1919, one evening he was told to attend a meeting of the German Workers Party and report its contents.

He became so interested that soon after the meeting he became member seven of the party. By 1921 he became its leader. It had become the National Socialist Party (NAZI and had adopted the 'Swastika' as its emblem. Now he was a great orator and made frenzied attacks on the Treaty of Versailles and Jews. His party's Storm Troopers now numbered 10,000 in 1923 and he decided to proclaim himself Dictator of Bavaria. One November 8 or November 9, he attempted a revolution in Munich. He was arrested and tried for treason. In prison he wrote his famous book 'Mein Kampf' (My Struggle). In 1932 Hitler had made his party the largest group in the Reichstag. President Hindenburg was compelled to appoint him Chancellor on January 30, 1933. In a referendum held in November 1933, 95% of the people voted approval of the new leader. Hence after the death of Hindenburg in 1934, Hitler assumed the presidency without any legal act or election. He took the title of Fuehrer and became an absolute dictator.

In violation of the Treaty of Versailles he built Germany into a first rank military power for the broad purposes of conquest. In 1937 he formed with Italy the Rome Berlin Axis. He annexed his native Austria on March 13, 1938. A year later he occupied Czechoslovakia and on March 23, 1939 he captured Memelland from Lithuania. On August 23 he agreed to a Non-Aggression pact with Russia. He invaded Poland on September 1, 1939. From this the World War II started. Poland surrendered.

The War began in earnest in 1940 as Hitler the Conqueror turned his eyes westward. In April he sent his troops into Denmark and Norway. May 10 marked the invasion of France, Holland, Belgium, and Luxembourg. In 1941 he took the Balkans and Greece. Then he committed a blunder: his gaze expanded further eastward to the Soviet Union. This led to a turning of the tide against him in 1943. After the attack on Pearl Harbor by Japan, the USA joined Britain and France. Germany was surrounded from all sides. Instead of surrendering, Hitler and his wife Eva committed suicide on April 30, 1945 leaving a permanent mark on world history.

Leaders like Hitler are born in thousands of years. Had he been just and kind to all races, he would have been treated like an angel. His extreme nationalism, hatred for Jews and other communities, and his belief in a master race made him a devil which haunts history forever.

CHAPTER NINE

Great Personalities: Liberators

Joan of Arc:

Joan of Arc is a French national heroine and one of the most popular saints of the Roman Catholic Church. She was a gentle peasant girl who led the soldiers to victory at the Siege of Orleans. She was born at Domremy, France, in 1412. She was not taught to read and write but learnt all that her mother could teach of sacred things. The innocent young maiden had many visions which she believed to be from Heaven. They led her to leave her family and go to the court of King Charles 7 of France, who was then uncrowned. It was likely that Charles wanted to embarrass her. She finally convinced him that she was to be the rescuer of France.

Charles clothed her in full armor and gave her a sword and banner. Joan mounted on a horse and led the French into battle. The Hundred Years War with England was for the succession of the French crown. Her courage and enthusiasm inspired the soldiers. They freed the city of Orleans in 1429. They defeated the English in four other battles and marched to Reims. There Charles was crowned the king of France in 1429. Joan of Arc stood by his side. After the end of her mission she wished to return to the little town of her birth. Charles would not consent. The valiant girl did not see victory again. She led an attack on Paris, her armor making her a shining mark for the English arrows. She was badly wounded. The Burgundies, who were French allies of the English, captured her on May 23, 1430. They sold her to the English for 1,600 Francs. The English were not satisfied merely with her capture. They feared her as much as the French admired her. She was put into prison for a long time. She was tried as a witch and a heretic. The court condemned her to be burned at the stake.

A martyr's death awaited Joan on May 30, 1431. Tens of Thousands of men stood in the marketplace at Reuben to watch her die. They saw the young maiden of Orleans face her death with high courage and turn her glance towards the blue sky. She was burned alive. Her ashes were thrown into the Seine River. The young martyr was pronounced innocent of charges against her in 1456. She was beatified by Pope Pius 10 in 1909. She was formally declared a saint in 1919. She was one of the rarest of rare women the world has ever produced. Her life and martyrdom show that even one person can change the destiny of a nation if they are true to their mission.

George Washington:

The people of the United States and other lands call George Washington the Father of the United States. He truly earned the title by looking after his country the way a good father would look after his child. He fought for his country and helped it to grow large and strong. He guided his people when he was young and helped to set up a wise and good government. In the history of the world very few people have done so much to help any country as Washington did to the USA.

Born on February 27, 1732 at a farm in Virginia called Wakefield, Washington grew up as a fine young man. He was once considered an experience colonial officer and asked to serve the British forces. He took part in the war against France at Fort Duquesne and earned fame.He got married in January 1759 to Martha Custis at the Custis Estate. In 1760s the British government began a much firmer policy towards the colonies and tried to extract as much money as possible. Washington did not like it. He was won over by the idea of resistance. The writings of Thomas

Pain and John Dixon made a great impression on him. He was ready to fight, if necessary, to protect the liberties to which he thought British subjects everywhere were entitles. After the famous Boston Tea Party the British placed Boston under military control. The American Resistance also started.

The First Continental Congress gathered in September 1774 at Carpenter's Hall near Philadelphia State House. Washington did not make a speech but moved among the delegates to get acquainted with them. The struggle against the British government had begun. In the Second Continental Congress John Adams proposed the name of Washington for commanding the forces of freedom fighters. Congress elected him to the office on June 15, 1775. The war started in right earnest. In July 4, 1776 congress adopted the document which proposed America Independent. Although the British had captured New York Washington won New Jersey. The Battle of Saratoga boosted the morale of Washington's troops; it convinced the world that America might win the war. In 1778 France entered the war on the American side. The tide began to turn. In the War's last battle American and French forces defeated the British at Yorktown and the British commander, Lord Cornwallis, surrendered before George Washington. America had won her freedom as recognized by Britain in the Treaty of Paris in 1783.

After the war Conservatives and Democrats began quarrelling. They ultimately ratified a constitution which paved the way for a Presidential form of democracy. Congress again turned to Washington to lead the nation. He was elected the First President of the United States, taking office on April 30, 1789 at the Federal Hall in New York. Those were highly critical times for the new nation. Since Washington enjoyed the faith of all, all matters were solved one by one. The Supreme Court of America was inaugurated in 1790. Three new states- Vermont (1791), Kentucky (1792), Tennessee (1796)- joined the USA paving the way for others.

Today the USA boasts the best roads in the world. It was started in Washington's second tenure. The first toll road was completed in 1794. The First Ten amendments were made in 1791. The revolutionary invention of the Cotton Gin, which made cloth available to even the poor, was made in 1793. Washington did not become a dictator and helped meetings with the Cabinet regularly, to firm up democracy within the country. National Mint was established in 1792. The first ever census was taken in 1792. In 1791 the plans were approved for the new capitol. His tenures were not free from problems though: debts had to be paid, and the Whiskey Rebellion against tax on liquor had to be tackled. On March 4 4,797, Washington retired from the public life. He had an unflinching love for his country.

When the French Directory threatened war, President Adams sent for Washington. He wore his military uniform again and came to Philadelphia for making plans and selecting officers for war. Good sense prevailed and war was avoided. He returned home in time for his birthday. On December 13, 1799 he went for a ride in windy and damp weather. He caught a cold and died on December 14, 1799. Thus a hero, first in war, first in peace, and first in the heart of his countrymen, left a rich legacy of democracy behind him.

Abraham Lincoln:

Abraham Lincoln is revered throughout the world for his concern about human dignity and martyrdom for his cause. He was the 16th president of the United Stated of America. Lincoln was born on February 12, 1809 on a farm near Hodgenville in the family of Thomas Lincoln. Long before Abraham came of age, he reached his full height of 6ft 4 in. He was thin and awkward, big boned and strong. His face was homely, his skin was dark, and his hair was black and course. From 1831 to 1837 he lived in a small village of Coles County, Illinois, working with Offutt. Soon the Black Hawk War broke out and Lincoln volunteered for the campaign. Others promptly elected him captain. In 1834 he was elected to legislature by a good majority. In legislature, he came quickly to the front. He was witty, ready in debate, and so skillful in management that he became the Whig floor leader.

This gave him his first chance to make a public statement of his attitude towards slavery. John T Steward inspired him to study law. Subsequently in 1836 he became a lawyer. He married Mary Todd on November 4, 1842. In 1843 he sought his party's nomination for congress but was not allowed. In 1846 he was elected to Congress. In 1854 he joined the Republicans and worked hard for the party. When the republican national convention met in Chicago in

May 1860, he got the Republican nomination for presidency which he won. On March 1861 he took the oath for the Presidency of the United States. Bickering among the states started on the question of slavery. During the presidential campaign the southern radicals had threatened that they would withdraw from the union if Lincoln were elected. One week after his inauguration, 11 southern states carried out their threat and seceded.

The Civil War started. During the war on September 22, 1862 he issued a preliminary. In it he declared that all slaves in the states of rebellion would be declared free when the Final Proclamation would be issued on January 1. The Union Forces were winning battle after battle. Lincoln was elected president for second term with a huge majority. He took the oath for the second time. On April 9, 1865 the Confederates surrendered. Lincoln had become a very popular figure by now, both home and abroad. On the night of April 14, 1865 he attended a performance of "Our American Cousin" at Ford's Theater. A few minutes after 10 PM, a shot rang through the crowded house. John Wilkes Boothe, a famous actor of the day, had shot the president in the head. He died at 7:22 on the morning of April 15, 1865.

Under his leadership the American Union was preserved. Only war made Lincoln believe more strongly that democracy is the best of all forms of government. After father of the nation George Washington, he is the most popular president. World leaders have taken inspiration from the emancipation of the slaves. They have paid rich tribute to his definition of democracy: "democracy is of the people, for the people and by the people".

Simon Bolivar- El Liberator:

Simon Bolivar has been hailed as El Liberator because he helped several South American countries achieve independence from Spain. He was born in Caracas, Venezuela in 1783. He died in Columbia in 1830. After studying in Madrid, Spain, Bolivar returned to Venezuela and led an uprising to drive out the Spaniards. He was then elected president of the new republic. He crossed the mountains into Columbia and drove out the Spanish forces from their too. After Francisco Miranda, first of liberators, the great Bolivar became known in the Latin America history as "El Liberator." He was aided by Jose De Sain Martin who helped drive the Spanish army out from Argentina, Chile, and Peru. Bolivar's lieutenant Antonia Jose De Sucre liberated Ecuador. He played a great role in the building of Panama Canal.

He brought the new nations together at Panama to consider and inter-oceanic canal among other topics. Earlier he had led a victorious march over the Andes Mountains from Venezuela to New Granada in 1819. Then those two countries were united under the name of "Columbia" and Bolivar became its president. He defeated the Spaniards at Carabobo and gained independence for Venezuela. The southern provinces of Peru formed a separate state in 1825. This was named "Bolivia" in the honor of the liberator. Bolivar drew up the constitution for the new republic. Soon afterwards he was falsely accused of wishing to make himself a monarch or perpetual dictator of the South American empire.

There was growing discord and his enemies plotted to kill him. The assassins almost succeeded at Bogota, Columbia in 1826. Bolivar failed to bring union and harmony to the parts of South America that he had liberated. He said bitterly, "I have ploughed in the sea." His plans to bring all the republics of the South American hemisphere into a sort of League of Nations resulted in the first Pan-American Conference at Panama in 1825. But nothing of importance came out of it. He was reelected president in Columbia but was forced to retire in 1830 when Venezuela separated itself from Columbia. He died at Santa Marta, Columbia, exiled and in poverty. He had spent most of his private fortune for the cause of liberty.

Bolivar's fame has grown steadily since his death. Several towns and cities both in the US and South America have been named in his honor. His affectionately remembered as the "George Washington of South America."

Mahatma Gandhi:

Mohan Das Karam Chand Gandhi (1869-1948) was a spiritual and political leader of modern India. He was born at Porbandar in western India. He took the degree of Bar at law from England and practiced law for 20 years in

South Africa where he was sent to defend a lawsuit in 1893. There he was treated very shabbily by the whites due to the policies of racial discrimination. He began a long fight for abolition of these policies. His method of resistance without fighting and disobedience to civil laws won him success in 1914. He returned to India and co-operated with the British government in World War I. But the massacre of Unarmed Indians in a public meeting at Jallianwala Bag in Amritsar by the British army on April 13th, 1919 enraged him and he began his long programmer to secure India's independence from the British rule.

He promoted the campaigns of passive resistance and civil disobedience. In 1921, 1931, 1942, he led mass movements in which millions of people thronged the jails. He taught that people should not accept injustice and resist it without violence. The British had imprisoned him six times for his political activities. Several times he went on hunger strikes to win several reforms. The British called these strikes "Political Blackmail," but were afraid to let Gandhi die lest he became a martyr. He lived a simple life of sage, on the level of the poorest peasant. His customary clothing was a loincloth of linen and he ate only to keep himself a live. He practiced most Hindu beliefs but did not believe in the caste system which he tried to make unlawful. He encouraged the development of simple Indian industries, especially the home-weaving of cloth.

He demanded independence in return for help against Japan in the World War II. His request was not granted. He ordered another civil disobedience movement. He and 200 of his supporters were put into prison but the movement did not stop. Millions of people went to jail and the British government in London felt the tremors. At last, on 15th August 1947, India became a free nation. But the partition of India (creating Pakistan out of India) spread communal riots and violence on a large scale. He set on a fast unto death and the violence stopped on the 4th day. He has just ended the fast, and on January 30, 1948, he was shot dead by an assassin.

His special method of non-violent resistance and self-sacrifice inspired the freedom fighters throughout the world to gain freedom and liberation for the downtrodden even from the most tyrant foreign rulers. Great international figures like Martin Luther King Jr. took inspiration from him. Even today he is the guiding mast for the suffering humanity. He is a light in the darkness.

Lenin- Vladimir Ilyich Ulyanov:

Lenin was the leader of the communist movement in Russia and the founder of the Soviet Union. He was born in Simbirsk (now Ulyanovsk) on the Volga River in 1870 in a quite ordinary family. In 1887 one of Lenin's brothers took part in a plot to take the life of the czar Alexander III and was hanged. This event deeply influenced Lenin. After doing law, he was admitted to the bar in 1891. He never practiced law seriously but became a professional revolutionary under the influence of Marx.

He moved to St. Petersburg (now Leningrad) in 1893 and became a member of a political group called "The Fighting Union for the Liberation of the Working Class." He was jailed in 1895 and exiled to eastern Siberia. In 1900 he was freed and went abroad where he became a leader of one faction of Russian party of social democrats. First in Munich and later in London, he and his friends published "Iskar" (The Spark) This revolutionary newspaper was smuggled back into Russia and had a great influence.

The revolution of 1905 brought Lenin back to Russia. He supported an armed revolt against the Russian government and establishment of the dictatorship of the working class (the proletariat). With the failure of the revolution, Lenin once more left Russia. Until 1914, he was active in Socialists Second International, a worldwide socialist organization. When the World War I broke out, he declared, "The transformation of the war into a civil war is the one good watchword for the working class." He told his followers that the workers of all the nations should stop fighting one another and rise against their rulers.

After the collapse of the czar's government in Russia in 1917, Lenin immediately decided to return to Russia. In St. Petersburg he found a condition of confusion. He rallied his followers and demanded an immediate end to the war, distribution of land among the peasants, and other measures. His program was called "crazy" and he was accused of being in the pay of the Germans. He was forced to hide in Finland. In October in 1917, the revolution broke out in St. Petersburg and spread quickly to Moscow and provinces. The Congress of Soviets took over the government. The newly formed counsel of the people's commissars was given the actual power. Lenin was at the head of this group. He was the directing force of the Soviet Government from this time until his death in 1924. He consolidated the disjointed country into a strong nation. He proposed a series of modifications to the drastic laws that were enforced. He had foreseen that his death the signal for a bitter struggle for mastery for the Soviet Government. For several years, there was a tug of war between various factions and personalities in the Communist Party. Joseph Stalin eventually won out as his successor. After Lenin's death, his body was embalmed and placed in a great tomb in Moscow. He became an inspiration to all the communists of the world. Although, communism is on its last leg, Lenin is still regarded as a great leader throughout the world. Revolutionaries in all the countries have taken inspiration from him.

Mao Tse-tung:

Mao Tse-tung was the most influential leader from the 1950s-70s in the world politics. He was born near Chang Sha in Hunan province in 1893 and educated at First National School there. He became interested in politics in the early 1920s. He read Marxist and Chinese Nationalist literature and agitated for support for the Chinese Nationalist Government Chiang Kai Shek. He became a communist and edited a party newspaper from 1924-196 but he was not popular with the party leaders because he advocated open revolution. He was dismissed from the party several times between 1927 and 1934. When the communists were forced to move their headquarters to northwestern China, the party leaders were discredited. Mau became the leader of the Chinese Communist Party at the new northern headquarters in Shensi province.

The communists and the nationalists were fighting a bitter civil war when the Japanese invaded China in 1937. They signed a truce and agreed to fight together against the Japanese, but they continued to fight each other as well. When the war with Japan ended, Mao's communist armies controlled all northern and western China. In the turmoil that followed, Mao gradually drove the nationalist forces to the south and the east until he controlled China's entire mainland. Chiang Kai Shek moved his government to the island of Formosa. In 1949, Mao was named "Chairman of the People's Republic of China" as the communists called their dictator-controlled country.

Under Mao, China got surrounded by an iron curtain. Its connection with the outside world was almost cut off. His expansionist designs grabbed Tibet- a buffer hill state between China and India. Its ruler and spiritual head, Dalai Lama had to flee to India with his followers. Mao put a claim on vast areas of India in Ladakh and northeast and ordered his forced to grab them. Consequently a bloody war was fought in 1962 between India and China. In Korea, Vietnam, Cambodia, Laos, and Indonesia, Mao spread his influence and harassed the western powers which viewed him with suspension.

Inside China, all revolts and dissent were suppressed mercilessly. By the mid-60s, all was quiet. Then he started the Cultural Revolution with an aim to modernize China. He, Chou-en-Lai, and Deng Xiaoping worked hard to make China one of the most powerful nations in the world. Mao's personality forced the USSR communism to leave the Asian field for him. In the 70s, China became so powerful that the US and its Allies were forced to acknowledge China as the rightful leader of the permanent seat in the UNO Security Counsel. Now Mao was the most powerful ruler in the world.

Under him China became a modern powerful nation. He remained active till his death on September 9, 1976. Very few people in the world have equaled him in leadership. Today's China owes everything to Mao who waged a war relentlessly against the enemies of China and emerged successful. Today China is the second largest economy of the world and perhaps and second most powerful nation in the world. Mao's dream has come true.

CHAPTER TEN

Events Which Changed the World

End of Egyptian Civilization:

World's oldest civilization flourished in the valley of the world's longest river Nile some 6,000 years ago. Its grandeur is evident everywhere in the valley. The Sphinx stretches its lion like body along the desert sand and looks silently towards the East, as it has for more than four thousand years. The Great Pyramids stand guard over the tombs of early rulers or pharaohs. Many pharaohs ruled Egypt before the Pharaoh Ramsay II mentioned in the Old Testament in the story of "The Great Exodus," which tells the adventures of Moses and his people. Magnificent ruins of beautiful temples at Abydos, the oldest city of Upper Egypt has a burial ground of earlier kings and the Egyptian god Osiris. The beautiful temples, built by Seti I (1313-1202 B.C.) and Ramsay II (1292-1225 B.C.) and the list of earlier kings carved on tablets attached to the walls of the temples, is a wonderful tale of great civilization. Equally important is Memphis, the ancient capital of Egypt founded about 3,400 B.C. by Menes, the first king to rule over the united Egypt. Thebes, the last capital of the splendid civilization from 1580-1090 B.C., is the home of Ammon or Amon-Ra, the highest god of the imperial period, including the villages of Karnack and Luxor on the east bank of the Nile tell their own story. A burial ground called the Valley of the Tombs of the kings on the west bank of the river with great temples built in 2000 B.C. stand even today. Beautiful and impressive in the splendor of their ruins coupled with the largest and the grandest temples of Queen Hatshepsut, Seti I, Ramsay II, Ramsay III, statues of Amenhotep III, the tomb of Tutankhamen or the Egyptian museum all announce the greatness of this ancient civilization.

Yet the tragic end of all this came not suddenly but gradually. It started around 1050 B.C. when conflicts and wars lasting up to 332 B.C. put a lid on the greatness. The ruler power weakened and governors and priests, especially Amun, became more powerful than ever. From 21st to 30th dynasty invasion and civil wars followed one after another. The Assyrians invaded Egypt 3 times. In 332 B.C., Alexander the Great conquered Egypt and declared himself a pharaoh. Throwing his white cap to the ground he indicated the sight of the future city of Alexandria. When he died in 323 B.C. one of his general became the rule of Egypt under the name of Ptolemy I and founded his dynasty. The era of the pharaohs was over. Egypt was Greek for 3 centuries until Cleopatra, the most beautiful woman of her time and the queen of Egypt, welcome Julius Caesar, the Roman general in 40 B.C. Egypt fell under the rule of Rome and never regained her earlier splendor.

The wheel of time had moved a full circle to show that nothing is immortal in this world.

Destruction of Carthage:

Carthage was one of the greatest cities of ancient times. It was famed for its size and its wealth, the great empire which it ruled and the extent of it trade. The city was situated on a peninsula of North African coast, 3 miles away from the site of modern Tunis. In legend, the city was set to have been founded by Dido, daughter of a Phoenician king of Tyre (Lebanon). Soon the Carthaginian warriors conquered other cities and lands. By 200 B.C. it had become one of the greatest cities of the time. It ruled the northern coasts Africa from what is now known as the Gulf of Sidra to the strait of Gibraltar. Sardinia and nearly the whole of a Sicily were under Carthaginian rule. People of southern Spain and Corsica kept themselves free only by paying tribute to Carthage. As early as 600 B.C., it was widely known as a warring city. Between 480 and 275 B.C., the Carthaginian tried repeatedly to take hold of Sicily from the Greeks. The strength of Carthage and its importance as a trading center worried the Romans after they conquered the southern part of Italy. Rome was rising in power, and nearby Carthage was looked upon as a dangerous rival. In 218 B.C., Hannibal's Carthaginian army invaded Italy. He crossed Pyrenees Mountains and the Alps with his soldiers riding on elephants. Rome feared his arrival, but Hannibal was not equipped to besiege Rome. The war dragged on and in the South of Italy and Carthaginian gradually weakened. In 2010 B.C. a young roman general, Scipio, was given the task of driving the Carthaginians out from Spain. Scipio captured Cartago Nova (now Cartagena) a fortified city. He then defeated Hannibal's brother Hasdrubal at Betula in 209 B.C. Thus, Spain fell under Roman control.

Scipio realized the only way to entice Hannibal from Italy, was to attack his home city and declare, "Carthage must be destroyed." His army of 30,000 men crossed into Africa and went from victory to victory. In 203 B.C., 60,000 Carthaginians died when his army set fire to two camps. Alarmed by Scipio's success, the Carthaginians recalled Hannibal. In 202 B.C. Hannibal was defeated at Zama, surrounded by Roman troops. Scipio imposed harsh terms on Carthage for peace. The city was made to give up its overseas possession and was forbidden to take any military action without authorization from Rome. It was also forced to pay indemnities in silver and surrender its elephants and galleys. Scipio returned in time to Rome. After a few years, Carthaginian power rose again. Finally in 146 B.C., the Romans captured Carthage. After a siege, which lasted for 2 years, the city was set ablaze and raised to the ground. After the destruction of Carthage, the surrounding country became a roman province. The roman emperor Augustus had Carthage rebuilt in 29 B.C. and the city once again began to grow and soon got its pristine glory. It was one of the greatest cities of the Roman Empire. In 439 A.D., it became the capital of the Vandal king Genseric. About 100 years later, Carthage became a part of Byzantine Empire under the Emperor Justinian. Carthage was finally destroyed by the Arabs in 698 and was not rebuilt. Today all the remains of the beauty and power of ancient Carthage lay in its tomb and ruins of its buildings.

End of the Roman Empire:

The Roman Republic ended with Julius Caesar. In 27 BC his nephew, Octavian, finally took power and he became the first emperor of Rome under the name Augustus. Under him the army became a body of professionals and a permanent service. With him started 'Pax Romana', peace of Rome. The word 'Rome' represented law as far as the Roman Empire expanded. About 116 AD the world saw the reign of the emperor Trajan who took the empire to its greatest expansion. The Mediterranean Sea became 'Roman Lake'. The empire covered a part of Asia, Europe, and Africa. Prosperity reached a great height in the rule of five good emperors: Nerve, Trajan, Hadrian, Antonius Pius, and Marcus Aurelius. The highest public offices in the state were thrown open to men of talent from the provinces. Hence no hereditary emperor. Marcus Aurelius was the first emperor to grasp the idea of 'One Father Land'. The empire was securely held inside its frontiers.

Rome faced and increasingly difficult military situation after 200 AD. Frequent problems on the borders, added expenses which had a series effect upon the economic structure, and increasing power of the army was giving trouble. For almost 100 years (193 AD to 284 AD) the army put the emperors in power and removed them at will. In one space of 67 years there were 20 emperors. Roman civilization in the west was fighting for its life. During this time Christianity was growing and spreading inside the empire. Great changes were taking place outside of the empire. A vigorous new Persian empire replaced the declining Parthian power. New and more powerful federations of German tribes formed the west. These tribes were forcing open the gates of the Roman Empire and were soon to burst into the European provinces.

Emperor Diocletian (245 AD -313 AD) decided that one man could no longer hold the entire empire together. He divided the state into East and West parts, to make it easier to govern. He chose a soldier named Maximillian to rule with him as joint emperor. New administrative reforms were done. In 306 AD Constantine the Great was proclaimed emperor of the west at York, Britain. He later made war on Licinius, who was the emperor of the east. After defeating him he made himself the master of the entire empire. In 313 AD Constantine established Christianity as the legal religion of the empire. He also moved the center of the government from Rome to the ancient city of Byzantium on Bosporus. A new capital was built there and named Constantinople. He left the left the Latin language and the priceless arts of law and government to the Christian church. He also gave to Constantinople the duty of preserving the ancient culture of Greece. After Constantine the Roman economy had weakened greatly dude to increasing army and a vast number of public employees. Farmers stopped farming due to heavy burdening taxes. In 410 A.D., the Germanic tribe 'Goths,' under Alaric, burst into Italy and swept on to Rome. The once mighty city was captured and looted. In 455 A.D. the same thing happened again. In 476 A.D., the last emperor Romulus was brushed aside by the German leader Odoacer who made himself the king of Italy. Thus the Roman Empire in the West collapsed. The Eastern Byzantine empire continued to grow in power and wealth under able rulers, like Theodosius I and Theodosius II. Emperor Justinian (527-565 A.D.) started the Golden Age of the empire. He was the last emperor to speak Latin. He was responsible for putting the Church under the power of the government. He published the final edition of Roman law which we now know as the 'Justinian Code.' After him, the empire started shrinking due to attacks of the Arabs, the Slavic, the Bulgarians, and the Lombard. Emperor Basil II tried to restore the glory. After his death, the Turks invaded. In 1453 A.D., Constantinople fell to the Ottoman Turks leaving the Roman Empire in the pages of history.

Ottoman Empire:

The Ottoman Empire was a great Muslim empire in the world in the 16th century. It was founded by Osman or Ottoman who became a leader of a band of Turks in 1289 A.D. In 1336 A.D., he captured Bursa. This date usually is given as the beginning of the Ottoman Rule. Orkhon, Osman's son organized the Ottoman possessions in Asia. The Byzantine emperor, John Cantacuzene, called on the Ottoman's for aid in a civil war, and the Turks crossed into Europe for the first time in 1345. Nine years later, they settled in the southwest of Constantinople. From this small beginning they rapidly spread throughout Thrace. They took Adrianople in 1360 AD calling it Edirne and made it their capital the next year. By the early 1400's the city of Constantinople was the only Christian land in a Muslim sea. The Turks finally captured the city under Mohammad II in 1453, amounting the formal end of the Eastern Roman Empire. Turks had already conquered Bulgaria and parts of Hungary. His troops marched on and captured a large part of the Balkans. By 1600 AD the empire had been extended into Asia and Africa. Constantinople had become Istanbul.

The Ottomans always spoke of their empire as a 'Great Tent', held up by the high officials. Under Salim I, grandson of Mohammad II, the Turks defeated Mameluke, the rules of Egypt, and took most of Arabia. The Ottoman Sultans took the title of Caliph, or spiritual leaders of Islam, after getting Egypt. The empire reached its heights under Salim's son, Suleiman I, called 'The Magnificent'. He ruled from 1520-1566 AD and concentrated his attentions on Europe. He conquered Hungary and three Europe into panic. Now the empire was controlling Asia Minor (Turkey, Balkans, Present day Iran, and part of Africa, Saudi Arabia, and Syria). He took active part in European politics. Five years after his death the empire started declining.

Turks were defeated at sea in the Battle of Nepanto. They made peace with Spain in 1585 AD. Sultans became pleasure seekers. Their Viziers took control. All through the 1700s the Turks fought defensively. In 1774 AD they were forced to open their waters to Russian ships. Another war with Russia, from 1787 to 1792, brought new Turkish losses. The empire suffered more and more loses during the 1800s and became 'The Sick Man of Europe'. It would had collapsed but European power (Austria France Britain and Prussia) did not want Russia to expand its influence all the way across the Mediterranean. They kept the empire alive. Turks had to give Russia the area between the Dnestr and Prut rivers in 1812. Greece declared its independence in 1821. A war with Russia on the side of Greece forced them to give Russia the control of the mouth of the Danube River by Adrianople Treaty in 1829.

Mehmet Ali of Egypt, who had helped the Turks against Russia, demanded independence of Egypt and control over Syria in compensation. He defeated the sultan. European powers saved the empire again from collapse. They fought in Crimean War on the side of the Ottoman Empire, defeating Russia in 1856. In the Russo-Turkish War of 1877-1878 Turkey was defeated. The Congress of Berlin, however, the European powers forced Russia to return a large power of the territory. Turkey lost Algeria to France in 1830, Tunisia in 1881. Cyprus in 1878 and Egypt in

1882 were lost to Britain.

In the First World War, Turkey took the side of Germany. It was defeated. The Sultanate was abolished. The empire was completely dismembered. Mustafa Kemal Pasha of the Young Turk Movement took over the leadership of Turkey and started the modernization.

The rise and fall of these great empires outline only one thing: all magnificent things, powerful rulers and big empires must collapse. They have the same end. As Thomas Grey has said in his famous elegy:

Boast of heraldry pump and power,
All that wealth and beauty ever gave
Await alike inevitable hours
Paths of glory leads but to grave

Hundred Years of War:

This struggle between England and France was a succession war and broken treaties. It extended over the reign of five English and French kings who fought over control of France. England claimed the lands of William of Normandy, who had conquered England in 1066. English and French fishermen and sailors quarreled over rights in the English Channel. Finally King Edward III of England, whose mother was the sister of three French kings, formally claimed the French crown in 1337 and began the war.

The course of war was hindered by Peasant Rebellion, Civil Wars in France, the Black Death, or Bubonic plague, and Peasant Rebellion in England. This development also began the decline of the feudal age. England won the greatest victory of the entire hundred years in the Battle of Crecy (1346) where French knights were slaughtered, killed by the first cannons to appear on battlefield, by archers and infantry. 19,000 English soldiers destroyed more than half of the French army of 60,000 men. Poitiers (1356) was another English triumph. The Treaty of Bretagne in 1360 marked a period of peace. Henry V of English, however, renewed the war, and was victorious at the Battle of Agincourt in 1415.

The Treaty of Troy, five years later, gave him the French crown. Upon his death (1422) the English claim to the throne was disputed and the war renewed. By 1428 the English had swept through northern France and laid siege to Orleans, gateway of central and southern France. The English seemed to have an upper hand. In 1429, the tide of battle was turned by Joan of Arc, a simple peasant girl, who led the French army to victory after victory. The greatest military achievement was raising the siege of Orleans (1429). Although she was captured and burnt alive by the English, France continued to win battles. By the time war ended in 1453, all the England had left on the continent was the Fort of Calais. The French did not get possession of this city until 1458. Thus the war in fact lasted more than 100 years. This war took a heavy toll on knights and led to the decline of feudalism. The use of gunpowder changed the future of war and made it more dangerous. It settled the succession dispute forever and set the rise of French Nationalism.

Renaissance:

'Renaissance' means re-birth in French. The name was made popular by a group of writers in the 1800s. These writers believed that the revival in Italy during the 1300s and 1400s of a study of ancient Greek civilizations marked the end of a period of ignorance and superstitions known as 'The Dark Ages'. So it was the rebirth of leaning. The word 'Renaissance' is misleading. During the so called 'Dark Ages' that is the Middle Ages, civilization made great strides upon which the later civilization has been squarely based. Thus Renaissance marks a shifting of emphasis rather than a rebirth of culture.

Renaissance implies the substitution of a worldly point of view for a religious point of view, with reference to art, literature, and the state. The center of reference became man, rather than God. This new attitude is called 'humanism'. The base upon which it rested was the gradual transfer of wealth and political power that went from the medieval church to modern territorial Princes'. Secondly the man of the renaissance sought a substitute for medieval society, based on religion, which they found in the societies of the past.They found the society they sought in classical culture of ancient Greece and Rome. The more intensive study of the Classics, therefore, was the natural consequence of the humanistic philosophy. It was a protest the clerical character of medieval education.

Beginning with Petrarch, Italian scholars turned away from the church dominated education to early century studies of Greek and Latin literature. Out of this change grew the kind of classical education that was common in Europe and American universities in the 1800s. At the same time, new styles developed in painting, sculptures, and architecture. All the arts became less and less influenced by religion. In some cases they turned for inspiration to classic models. The Renaissance in art spread from Italy to Flanders. Soon the movement was felt in most of Western Europe. The influence of Greece and Rome is especially seen in the buildings and monuments of the period. However, Renaissance architecture is even more remarkable for its new elements which are not classified at all. In the same way Renaissance paintings are distinctly original instead of merely copies of the masterpieces of antiquity. The same thing holds true in the field of literature.

In a larger sense the Renaissance was the early cultural expression of a new age, which emphasized the supremacy of the civil authority and prime importance of natural man. It developed in the age of Enlightenment, which preceded and prepared the way for the French Revolution. It brought about the end of feudalism and growth of cities. The use of gun powder revolutionized the methods of raising war. Modern science began. People started working with facts to overthrow superstition. The voyage to the oriental region by Vasco De Gama and others gave Europe luxury goods. These goods resulted in exploration and discovery. The invention of moveably print and the development of national languages quickly spread new ideas to all parts of Europe. The revival of Greek and Roman culture drew students to great centers of learning. This resulted in the establishment of universities and a general improvement in methods of academic education. Finally, new religious beliefs came because of free thinking. The rise of nationalism lessened the authority of Rome and helped the Reformation.

Reformation:

Reformation was a religious movement of the 1500s which resulted in the establishment of Protestantism. One of the most important leaders of this movement was Martin Luther, a German monk and scholar. The rebellion against the spiritual powers of the church was also a rebellion against is worldly power. For a thousand years the church had held an important place in the daily life of people. The Popes were the supreme authority over most worldly rules. The church was the main source of charity, education, and art. Few questioned their divine authority. It was well known that many of the church men abused their powers and cared little for the spiritual welfare of people. Masses of the people had been suffering from bitter poverty. The kings and nobles had plundered and abused them to carry on wars. The modern spirit of nationality was slowly breaking down the power of the Holy Roman Empire. Some of the rulers in Europe began to look jealously at the wealth and power held by the church. Due to the revival of learning University and schools sprang up everywhere. The church then lost the monopoly on education. Many reformers and protestant leaders came from the ranks of former church students. Among them were Wycliffe in England, Huss in Bohemia, Erasmus in Holland, Luther and Melanchthon in Germany, and Zwingli and Calvin in Switzerland.

It started in Germany with Martin Luther nailing his 95 Thesis on the door of this church. They were a protest on the practice of selling indulgences, or spiritual pardons. In 1519 he denied the authority of Pope Leo 10. The Pope issued a Papal order threatening to excommunicate Luther. In 1520 Luther publicly burned these documents in Wittenberg. He was summoned before the court and told to withdraw his heresy. He defied the church and the Pope, appealing to the authority of the scriptures to support his stand. Many German Princes were hostile to the demands of the Pope and accepted Luther's religious point of view. In 1530 they signed the Confession of Augsburg. This document is a fundamental statement of Lutheran Faith. Meanwhile a similar movement towards separation from the Catholic Church was going on in Switzerland under the leadership of Huldrych Zwingli. He was killed in civil wars. Swiss Cantons gained the right to choose their own religion. A new leader, John Calvin, appeared in Geneva.

Although he was exiled, students took his message to all parts of Europe. In France and Spain the rulers had already become quite independent of the Pope. They did not expect and gain by supporting Protestantism. In France,

Calvin's teachings were taking root. His followers were called Huguenots. On Saint Bartholomew's day in 1572 thousands of them were murdered. In 1523 Sweden broke away from its union with Denmark and Norway. Men who had studied under Luther himself had brought a new faith northward. In Sweden the new king saw Protestantism as a good way to become independent of the church. Norway and Denmark also followed it in 1536.

Henry VIII of England quarreled with the Pope over his right to divorce his wife and remarry. He announced in 1534 that he, and not the pope, was the head of the English church. Thus Protestantism became chief religion of the countries of Northwestern Europe. To contain Reformation the church started the Counterreformation within the church. It took three directions. Reforms were made in the church and in clergy. A great education campaign was carried on by a catholic order, the Jesuits. Inquisition was used as a method of suppression. In this way the reformation movement had far reaching effects in religious, political, and social life in Europe.

Colonization of South America:

South America is the fourth largest Continent on the globe. It takes up nearly 1/7 of the land area in the world. South America, together with Mexico and countries of Central America, is sometimes called Latin America. Many of the people speak either Spanish or Portuguese, which are Latin languages. They follow the customs of the Latin countries of the old world. Before the coming of the Europeans some of the South American countries had developed a high degree of civilization. Aztec civilization of Mexico and Inca civilization of Peru were prominent. They were skillful builders and goldsmiths and had a sophisticated system of agriculture and irrigation. They were isolated, however, from the rest of the world. They had built bigger pyramids than those of the Egyptians. Complex citied like Machu Picchu among high mountains together with the colossal statues of the Sun god and temples of Quetzalcoatl could be found among these civilizations,

In the 15th century Portugal and Spain, once prominent power of Europe, became paupers due to continuous wars. After the discovery of the American continents in 1492 by Columbus both Spain and Portugal wanted to claim land in South America but avoid a war at the same time. They therefore request Pope Alexander VI to decide who would control the lands that European sailors were exploring. Fernandez and Isabella of Spain wanted King John II of Portugal to give Spain rights over many of these territories. The Pope issued his ruling by drawing an imaginary line around the world. It was called the 'Line of Demarcation'. Portugal could claim all known Christian lands to the East of the line and Spain to the west of the line. After some adjustment the Treaty of Tordesillas was signed in 1494 and the way of colonization opened for spreading Christianity, expanding empires, and becoming richer.

Sprain began its conquest of the Americas. Soldiers called Conquistadores explored the Americas and claimed them for Spain. Hernando Cortes landed on the Central American coast with 508 men in 1519. His arrival shook the Aztec empire. The Emperor Montezuma feared that Cortes had been sent by the Aztec God to rule Mexico. He sent him gifts which included two disks of solid gold and silver. This increased the greed of Cortes. He put one faction against the other in 1521 he destroyed the Aztec Empire. Native American storied of Incas wealth reached Spain. This powerful empire was centered in the Cuzco Valley in what is now Peru. In 1531 a conquistador named Francisco Pizarro led an expedition of 180 men into Peru. Like the Aztecs, the Incas feared that the Spanish might be Gods. The Incan emperor Atahualpa ordered his troops not to fight. He gave Pizarro a treasure of gold. The Spaniards hanged him. With Atahualpa dead, the Incan empire collapsed in 1534. Pizarro took control of this area for Spain and called it Peru. His companion Diego De 'Almagro carried the Spanish far into Chile. In 1534 Sebastian Benalcazar conquered the land of present-day Ecuador. Junenez De Quesada conquered what is not Colombia between 1536 and 1538. In 1534 Pedro De Mendoza led the colonizing expedition into the Plata River region and colonized Paraguay. In 1541 Francisco De Orellana crossed the might Andes from the Pacific Coast and followed the Amazon River. Portuguese started exploring from East to West. In 1531 they began the exploration of Brazil and finally occupied the entire country. Spain and Portugal thus colonized most of South America.

The Rise and Fall of the British Empire:

It is said that the British Empire was founded at sea and that 'The Sun never sets on it'. The empire was a chain of countries and colonies stretching all the way around the globe. In the late 1500s during the reign of Queen Elisabeth I English warships attacked Spanish ships and colonies around the world. The English navy and merchant men from British ports explored vast areas of the world in the search of new riches. The East India Company was founded in 1600s to develop trade between Britain and the East Indies. The Hudson Bay Company was founded in 1670 to explore Northern Canada. French and British sectors fought wars in Canada until France finally gave up its claims in the country in 1763. British and Dutch merchant men fought for the East Indies and other islands in the Pacific Ocean. British, French, Dutch and Portuguese colonists fought for the control of the riches of India until the British won at the Battle of Plassey. Many New colonies throughout the world were added to the empire during the Napoleonic wars of Europe in the early 19th century.

Some of the colonies of the empire were added as the result of exploration. The British explorers extended British influence from Egypt to the Cape of Good Hope in Africa. British government slowly took over control in these areas. After the revolt of 1857 the government took over India from the East India Company and made it part of the empire. The American colonists rebelled in 1776 because they were not given enough control over their government. Britain was forced to give local self-government to Nova Scotia before the American colonies won their independence in the Revolutionary War.

Canadian and Australian colonies were soon given some measures of self-independence. A great step forward was taken when Canada became a dominion in 1867. In the first years of the 1900s Australia, Newfoundland, New Zealand, and South Africa all were made dominions. They developed their own governments and elected their own assemblies. British parliament still controlled foreign affairs and defense of the entire empire. After World War I the British began to recognize that dominions were ready to become independent nations. Equal rights for the dominions in the newly established Britain Commonwealth of Nations were recognized at the Imperial Conference of 1926.

At that time the empire was still in control of 70 countries all around the world in all continents and oceans. They existed from Canada to New Zealand. World War II left Britain very weak. USA pressed it to free the countries. Russian influence in world affairs was increasing and almost all countries and territories were going through nationalist movements. British rulers thought it wise to dismantle the empire and have all of them in a Commonwealth so that friendly relations might ensure trade. India was first to be freed in 1947. In the 1950s and 1960s almost all countries in Asia and Africa were to follow. The British Empire has been completely dismantled. A good and friendly relationship with almost all these countries is an achievement of the Commonwealth.

The American Revolution:

The American Revolution, the conflict by which the American colonists won their independence from Great Britain and created the United States of America, was on upheaval of profound significance in the history. It took place in the second half of the 18th century. In 1763, the colonists were an expending and maturing people; their numbers had reached a million and half and they were doubling every quarter of the century. They could boast of five urban centers, "Cities in wilderness – Philadelphia, Boston, New York, Charleston, and New Port- serving as filters through which new ideas of new European enlightenment entered the 13 British colonies." Still there was no meaningful American nationalism.

After 1763, they felt endangered in the British Empire when the British government acted with a lack of sensitivity, ignoring the concern of its maturing subjects. To obtain more revenue due to rising national debts, the London government attempted too much too quickly. In 1759, disputes broke out between Britain and the colonies over disallowances of measures passed by the popular assemblies. They were Writs of Assistance, empowering the royal custom officials to break into homes and stores and over judicial tenure in colonial courts. It also forbade western settlement beyond the Appalachian Mountains (eliminating the paper currency as legal tender, bolstering the customs department, and enlarging the authority of vice admiralty court).

These unpopular measures were followed by Parliament placing taxes on Americans for the first time without American representation. The Sugar Act along with the Stamp Act placed taxes on sugar and all legal documents including newspapers. Also, the Quartering Act required colonists to provide troops with temporary housing.

Americans believed that they could be taxed only by their own directly elected representatives. As a retaliatory measure, they started boycotting British trade goods. Tension continued. In the meantime, on 5th March 1770 in Boston, on being taunted, the British soldiers fired indiscriminately into the crowd killing 3 colonists and mortally wounding 2 others. This Boston Massacre filled the Americans with anger and suspicion. Then the Tea Act, which allowed the British East India Company to bypass middlemen and sell directly to American retailers, was interpreted to drink taxed tea at a lower price.

The discontentment fomented and in Massachusetts capital the famous 'Boston Tea Party' resulted in the destruction by patriots of 340 tea chests on ships in the harbor. Harsh measures were taken to suppress this mini revolt. The other colonies rallied behind Massachusetts in the Continental Congress at Philadelphia in September 1774. The British reacted by sending 3,000 troops. Hostilities erupted at Lexington and Concord on April 19, 1775. The battle of Bunker Hill was fought on Breed's Hill on June 17, 1775. The second Continental Congress chose as commander of the army George Washington, a 43-year-old delegate from Virginia. The war continued. The colonists declared their independence on July 4, 1776.

The war continued for seven years (1775-1783). At last Britain recognized their independence by the treaty of Paris in September 1783. The new nation came into being in 1788. On April 17, 1789 George Washington became the countries first president. This was a struggle to preserve and expand the dimensions of human freedom and gave birth to an anti-colonial movement, the first of its kind. It gave birth to a new nation- a republic born in a revolution in war, a pattern followed by scores of fledgling states.

French Revolution:

The French Revolution, the most important event of Europe in the later part of 18th century, had far reaching effects throughout the world. It began when the French Emperor Louis 14 called the Estates General to provide money for the bankrupt government in 1789 and ended when Napoleon Bonaparte became the first consul of France. French commerce was growing rapidly in the 1700s and a class of merchants and manufacturers was becoming rich. The country was still in the Middle Ages, however, in its form of government and social organization. The king rules by 'Divine Right'. Nobles lived lives of great luxury while the peasants did not have enough to eat. The greater part of the tax burden was carried out by the lower and middle classes.

At the same time new ideas about freedom and government were spreading. The writing of Rousseau and Voltaire were influencing the people. The middle class felt hampered by ancient legal, political, and religious institutions. This class began to organize the people and to prepare for a revolution. When Louis 16 demanded money, his ministers advised him to make sorely needed reforms. He refused, which brought the country on the verge of revolution. French monetary help in the American Revolution left the treasury empty in 1787. Parliament, or high court, was to call the Estates General- the French national assembly- last called in 1614 on May 5, 1789. Until now the clergy, nobles and middle class had 1 vote each. The first two could get anything passed.

The third estate (middle class) refused to accept this voting pattern and demanded 1 vote-1 man. They boycotted and held a separate meeting in the tennis court and took oath that they would not Disband until France had a constitution. It was known as the Constituent Assembly and Tennis Court Oath. The king was forced to recognize them. A disgruntled king dismissed his chief minister and intended to dismiss the assembly. The people of Paris rose on July 14 and stormed the Bastille prison to secure arms. They murdered the governor of the prison and set the prisoners free. In October, a crowd of Paris women invaded the Royal Palace at Versailles. The royal family took the protection of the National Guards. During the next two years the National assembly passed laws which wiped out many abuses of the old feudal system and included the declaration of the rights of man on August 27, 1789 which made France a constitutional monarchy.

The King did not accept the acts of the assembly. In June 1791 he tried to escape from France with his family but was caught. Leaders suspected him of plotting against France with escaped nobles and foreign kings. The New Assembly, with its most radical group 'Mountain, Gironde', had speakers like Robespierre, Danton, Marat, and

Desmoulins. France was plunged into war against Prussia and Austria in April 1792. The early losses made people suspicious that the king was plotting against the country. In August 1792 the mob broke into the Royal Palace and imprisoned the king and his royal family. He was dethroned. More losses lead to the September Massacre in which thousands of aristocrats were killed.

The French army finally won. The two groups "Gironde and Mountain" began struggling for power. This was the most terrible state of the revolution. The royal family was executed. Then the revolution started eating up its own children. All its leaders were killed. The great blood bath continued. Finally Napoleon Bonaparte took over the French government and revolutionary fervor ended. The Revolution did not make France a democracy but rather a limited monarchy. It gave the world a loud message about people's power.

Russian Revolution:

The Russian Revolution of 1917 is the second important event of the first quarter of the 20th century that affected the whole world. People saw a new type of government come into play, curbs on individual freedom and expansions of the state's power, creation of power blocks resulting in a long, cold war. Russia had been a monarchy for centuries. The Czars were as autocratic as the Bourbons of France, or Tudors of England. The first revolution in the 20th century came in 1905, just after Russia lost Russo-Japanese war. This disaster in the Far East gave political rebels and agitators something new to talk about.

On Bloody Sunday, January 22, 1905 Grand Duke of Vladimir ordered the order guards to fire upon a procession of Saint Petersburg strikers and their families. They were led by an orthodox priest, Father Capon, bearing a petition to the 'little father' as the czar was affectionately called. Nearly 1,500 men women and children were killed. This cruel incident angered the Russians. The Social Democratic Labor Party had been formed in Russia in 1898 with the Marxian progeny. The party aimed to win support of its workers by means of party cells, or secret groups in the factories throughout Russia.

The Mensheviks and the Bolsheviks, the two groups of the party, differed on the methods. The former wanted to give up violence and terrorism and cooperate with all democratic parties for gradual improvement of worker conditions. The later led by Vladimir Lenin was more violent in its approach. These revolutionary groups had called a general strike in 1905. Water and electric supply were cut off in some countries. In the cities the revolutionaries established Soviets, the counsel of workers. The government pressure compelled Lenin to flee to Finland. In World War I, Germans forced Russia to retreat from Poland. By March 1917 it was clear that Czar Nicholas II and his government could not manage military affairs.

Riots broke out in Saint Petersburg for lack of food supplies. On March 12 the Czar was forced to abdicate. The Duma then set up a provincial government. The leaders of the Social Democratic Workers Party paid no attention and organized the Petrograd soviet of workers and soldiers 'deputies. When it appeared in Saint Petersburg with the help of Germans the second all Russian congress of Soviets, which met at Petrograd in November 1917 showed a Bolshevik majority. Lenin was quick to take advantage of this majority. Leon Trotsky was elected president of this congress. The Communist Party won control of Petrograd garrison. On the night of November 7, 917 (October 25 by the Russian calendar of the time) the Bolsheviks used troops to seize the government offices. In the morning when the Congress of Soviets met, the Bolsheviks were in control of the entire government. Street fights soon gave the Bolsheviks command of the capital.

A few days later the Bolsheviks won Moscow and extended the revolution into provinces. They lost no time in proclaiming Red Terror against the enemies of the Communist dictatorship. A civil war broke out and continued till 1920. Then Lenin became the dictator of the country and Russia became the Union of Soviet Socialist Republic and the first communist country. With planned economies, the country began to progress. The expansionist designs continued and, in the years, to come, neighboring countries of Estonia, Lithuania, and Latvia were absorbed. The whole of Eastern Europe: Hungary, Poland, Bulgaria, Czechoslovakia, East Germany, Yugoslavia (which withdrew in 1948) became Russian Satellites. After the Second World War the USSR vied with the USA in every field for the next 50 years.

Chinese Revolution:

China, the most populous country of the world, was once the most powerful empire in the East from 1500 B.C. to the middle of the 19th century. It developed a great civilization under the Shang, Chou, Ch' in, Han, Sui, Tang, Sung, Yuan, Ming, and Ch'ing dynasties. The Open-Door Policy of the late 19th century brought Europeans and Americans to China. In 1911, the monarchy was replaced by republic under Sun Yat Sen who died in 1925 leaving the field Chiang Kai Shek. Communists were at the loggerheads with the Nationalists' of Chiang. General was on firm footings. Northeastern provinces of China, which make up Manchuria, appealed to the Japanese as a rich prize. The Japanese army declared to stop the Chinese Republic before it became too powerful. On September 18, 1931 they started a fight which continued until it became a part of World War II. Japan captured Manchuria and made it a puppet state. The Chiang government conceded Japanese demands to buy time. By that time, the Communists had established them in Shensi province. With great efforts of Chang Hsueh-liang of Manchuria, a truce was reached between the government and the communist forces and they decided to drive away the Japanese from the Chinese soil. During WWII, China joined the Allies on January 1, 1942.

Consequently, the US and Britain gave up their extra-territorial rights in China. Chiang Kai Shek played a great role in persuading President Truman and British Prime Minister Attlee to atomize Japan to seek her surrender. It worked. Soviet troops had taken northeast China from Japan in the closing days of World War II. When the Russian troops withdrew in April 1946, Chinese communist troops quickly occupied key cities in the area. Fighting broke out at many places between the Communists' and the Nationalists' forces. American efforts for peace came to naught. The US supported the Nationalists' government with more than 2 billion dollars in aid. On April 1, 1947 the Nationalist Party, The Democratic-Socialist Party, and the Young China Party signed a mutual agreement which ended the one-party rule by the Nationalists. The first general election in China's history was held on November 21, 1947 and Chiang was elected President. The Communist troops aided by the Soviet Union won battle after battle against the Chinese government forces. On August 23, 1949, Nanking the capital fell to the Red forces. Chiang's government withdrew to Formosa Island but continued to fight the Communist with several hundred guerilla troops in the remote areas of China.

In September 1949, the Communists set up a government with its capital at Peiping. Mao Zedong became the Communist dictator of China. Most of the countries, including Britain and India, recognized the new government but the USA did not and the Nationalist government at Formosa retained its permanent seat in the UNO. With this revolution, a reign of terror started. Millions of opponents were killed in slave labor camps. A bamboo curtain was put on the outflow of news. After suppressing the opponents they started military buildup and soon, expansionist designs became clear by 1955. First the Communists invaded Tibet, an autonomous hilly state between India and China. The Tibetan ruler and religious head Dalai Lama fled for life to India. Before that the Chinese forces helped the Communists in fighting the UN forces in Korea. Later, the same method was repeated in Vietnam. Infiltration on Indian borders resulted in a war with India. In the mid-60s, Cultural Revolution took China to modern ways. By the 1970s, China had become so powerful that even the USA recognized and gave it the permanent seat in the UNO soon. After that Mao and Deng Xiao Ping started modernization. Today, China is the second most powerful and forward-looking nation. It is thought that if this state of things continues China may surpass the USA in economy and power.

Formation of the UNO:

After WWI, the US president, Woodrow Wilson, had dreamed of a world organization which would stop further wars and save mankind from its holocaust. The League of Nations was established in 1919 by the Treaty of Versailles to fulfill his cherished dream. It sought to guarantee peace and international security by preventing wars. The founders sought greater openness among the states and more co-operation among nations. But the USA, reluctant to be involved in European matters, refused to be a member of the league. In 1933, Germany left it to rearm itself. The league was doomed. Six years later, WWII broke out. In practice, the League of Nations lacked the means to be effective. The WWII left a deep and permanent scar on human psyche. In the last years of war, the charter of the UNO developed from proposals agreed upon at a conference held at Dumbarton Oaks estate in Washington D.C. and was attended by delegates from the USA, Great Britain, France, Soviet Union, and China.

On April 25, 1945, 1400 representatives from 46 nations met in San Francisco for a conference on an international organization. The Dumbarton Oaks proposals were put before the conference and the charter was signed after amendments were made. The UNO formerly came into existence when the ratified charter was placed with the US Department of States on October 1945. The first aim of the UNO is to maintain world peace. Its second purpose is to develop friendly relations among nations, "Based on respect of the principles of equal rights and self-determination of peoples. The UNO seeks also to achieve international cooperation in solving international economic, social, cultural, and humanitarian problems. It strives to promote respect for human rights and for fundamental freedoms for all. Finally it acts as a center where nations may need to discuss their problems and try to find solutions.

It is based in New York and the secretary general looks after day to day affairs. He is elected after every 5 years by the general assembly, assembly of all member nations (current number 209). Trygve Lie of Norway was the first secretary general. Among other matters discussed by the UNO in 1946 were evacuation of Soviet troops from Iran and withdrawal of French and British troops from Syria and Lebanon. It also asked all other nations to permit women the same political rights as man. An International Children's Emergency Fund was up to be used in countries that were victims of aggression. The UNO first discussed the Palestine problem in 1947 and as a result the UK gave up its mandate over Palestine in May 1948. The war between the new state of Israel and Arabs broke out.

An armistice was sponsored by the UNO. Fighting had broken out between the Netherland forces and the Republic of Indonesia in 1948. A committee was set up which arranged a truce and in 1949, both sides agreed to stop fighting. The UNO acted in 1948 to prevent war between India and Pakistan over Kashmir. An economic commission was set for Latin American countries in 1948. In 1949, it enabled Russia and the USA to lift the Berlin Blockade and reach an agreement. In 1950s, it stopped the Korean War from taking a monstrous shape. The same happened in the decades to come. Arab- Israel, India-Pakistan, Congo, Vietnam, Yugoslavia, Iran-Iraq, Ethiopia- Somalia, any of these disputes could have assumed a dangerous proportion. But the UNO has acted as a safety valve.

Independence of India:

India was a craze with the west for its riches and cultural heritage. It is well-known that Christopher Columbus had set out on a voyage in the 15th century to discover a sea-route to India and reached America and his compatriot, Vasco de Gama finally reached India. This early contact culminated in the arrival of the Dutch, the French, the Portuguese, and the British on the soil of India, ostensibly, for trade. The political bickering among Indian rulers encouraged them to harbor political ambitions. These European companies in a cut-throat competition tried to see the other out. They played with the rulers. Finally the British proved smarter and stronger. Gradually, taking the advantage of the weakness of the Indian princess, they played one against another.

Marathas were encouraged to subdue Tipu Sultan, whom they killed in the last Mysore War. Marathas were suppressed with the help of the Nizam, who himself was compelled to surrender before them. In the battle of Plassey (1787) Clive, by using cunningness and deceit, defeated and killed Sirazuddaula of Bengal and the very next year, using the same tactics, defeated the combined forced of the Mughal emperor Shah Alam, Nawab of Awadh Shuzauddaula and Mir Kasim, the Nawab of Bengal, at Buxur in Bihar. Thus, the British became the masters of India in garb of the British East India Company. It is really a wonder that a few thousand British soldiers enslaved 300 million Indians. Then started the exploitation of India and her interests were made subservient to that of Britain. Then a reaction started.

The people and princess rose against the British rule in 1857 in a big way. The first war of independence continued for more than 2 years until its leaders, Mughal Emperor Bahadur Shah, Peshwa Nana sahib, Laxmi Bai, Rani of Jhansi, Tatya Tope, the captain of these forces, were killed or exiled. According to crude estimates, 100,000 people were killed in this uprising. The British were able to suppress it with the help of other princes who were loyal to them. But it left a deep scar on Indian psyche. Religious preachers, like Swami Dayanand, Keshav Chandra Sen, and Swami

Vivekanand had reminded the people of the pristine of their culture. Revolutionary groups started violent activities, targeting the British and government property. In 1911, a bomb was hurled on the procession of Viceroy in Delhi. Several revolutionaries- Savarkar, Bhai Paramanand, and hundreds of others were deported to Andaman.

Many them were hanged but these violent activities did not stop. Bhagat Singh and his group threw a bomb in the Parliament in Delhi to draw the attention of the world towards India's plight. They were arrested and hanged. By now the time for non-violent mass movement has come under the leadership of Mahatma Gandhi. In Jallianwala Bag, Amritsar, Punjab, hundreds of people were shot when they were listening to the speeches of the leaders on April 14, 1919. This was followed by turmoil in the form of violent activities and the first great mass movement, "Non-Cooperation Movement."

This was withdrawn by Gandhi when it became a bit violent at places. This was followed by repression. But the ball had been set rolling. Non-violent movement in the form of Salt Movement, Farmer's Movement, and Quit India Movement continued under the leadership of Jawaharlal Nehru, Sardar Patel, and others. Subhash Chandra Bose founded the Indian National Army with the help of Japan in Burma during WWII and the army marched in the east. The Navy also revolted. The end of WWII made Britain so weak that it had to grant independence to India August 15, 1947 after breaking it into two parts that is India and Pakistan.

Rebirth of Israel:

Moses led the Jews to the Promised Land in Canaan in about 1200 BC according to the Old Testament of the Bible. The kingdom was founded in Israel by Saul, who was succeeded by David (1010-970 BC). Solomon (970-133 BC), the son of David and Bathsheba, became a great ruler. After his death the kingdom was divided into two- the northern kingdom (Israel) and the southern kingdom (Judah). In 722 BC Israel was invaded by Assyrians who exiled the 28,000 Jews. Judah survived until 597 BC when Nebuchadnezzar the great emperor of Babylon enslaved it. Ten years later Jerusalem was destroyed and most of the Jews were taken to Babylonia as slaves. In 539 BC Persian emperor Cyrus the Great captured Babylon and allowed the Jews to return from exile. Jerusalem could not live in peace, however. First Egyptians, then Syrians, and finally Roman general Pompey captured Jerusalem in 63 AD. The Jews revolted in 70 AD. After suppression of the revolt Jerusalem was razed to the ground and the Jews became refugees. They settled in ghettos wherever they found shelter. The rise of Christianity increased their persecution as the death of the Christ was attributed to them. They were barred from public offices and excluded from agriculture and business.

To make a living many Jews became pawn brokers and bankers who charged interest on loans. The charging of interest was regarded a sin by Christian and Muslim religions. They were also criticized for their closed society. Their unity and trade improved their economic condition in Western Europe. However their persecution continued in Eastern Europe. In the 1930s the ascendency of Hitler in Germany brought these persecutions to a new height. Hitler hated them so much that wherever the German army went, they rounded up the Jews and sent them to concentration camps for death by Gas Chambers. During the Second World War in his whim to wipe out the Jewish race Hitler killed six million Jews. The Zionist movement started in America. Its leader David Ben-Gurion declared that the Jews would get their homeland, Israel, for safety from further persecution. After the war the Jews from other parts of the world started purchasing land in Palestine. The Jews started migrating to Palestine in large numbers. At the time it was a British Mandate.

Halfheartedly Britain tried to stop this immigration but failed. In 1948 an independent Jewish state of Israel was pronounced with the connivance of the USA and Britain. Soon it was recognized by the western countries. Some of the Arabs who had been settled on the land for the last 2,000 years were forced into exile. This area of the Middle East soon became a hotbed for international turmoil. The Arab countries did not recognize Israel and the wars between Israel her neighbors (such as the War of 1948, 6 days War of 1967 and Yom Kippur in 1973) caused great bitterness. Terroristic attacks in Israel and Palestine have become day to day affair. America is trying to broker peace between them. Peace however has been elusive. It is also a fact that Israel must come to stay.

Vietnam War:

Vietnam is an important rice growing country in Indochina, South Eastern Asia. It has an area of 127250 sq miles. It is a long narrow land bordered by China in the north. It includes three former states of Tonkin, North Vietnam, Annam (Central Vietnam), and Cochin China (South Vietnam). The Truce agreement signed in July 1954, to end the fighting in the Indo-China war divided Vietnam into two sections, at a line formed by Ben Hai River just north of the 17th parallel. The Northern part included French Indo-China's former capital Hanoi. It was put under the control of the Communist Vietminh, headed by Ho Chi Minh. The Southern part became an independent country headed by Ngo Dinh Diem, an anti-communist leader. Much fighting against the government took place in South Vietnam. The rebels, the Viet Cong, were aided by China and North Vietnam. They tried taking control of the South. It was resented by the USA, which tried to persuade Hanoi to keep off. It was to no avail.

The fighting became fierce in the early 1960s. Fearing that the communist would spread throughout South East Asia, President Eisenhower and later Linden B. Johnson sent military advisors to help South Vietnam ward off the invasion from the North. In an American inspired coup the unpopular Diem was killed. New attacks on American warships on the Gulf of Tonkin led the United States to send the first combat troops into the country. With the American troops the fighting became fiercer and their involvement increased. Hanoi was bombed several times. Although the rebels were pursued into the North the Viet Cong were successful in generating hatred towards the American forces in the southern part of Vietnam. Even in the deep interior they gained sympathy. Some US soldiers committed cruelties. The communist bloc launched venomous propaganda throughout the world and painted the USA as a great villain after the My Lai Massacre in 1968. American soldiers were fighting the Vietnam War bravely but due to lack of cooperation casualties kept mounting. At home the American government faced stiff opposition. There were demonstrations all around the country and a demand to withdraw the forces gained momentum. It became an upheaval task for President Nixon to continue with this war. In a bid to improve relations with China he undertook a trip to the Communist land. He withdrew the troops in 1973 after heavy losses in both man and material. Soon the Vietminh took control of South Vietnam. In 1976 the reunited country became the Socialist Republic of Vietnam, with Ho Chi Minh Nagar Hanoi its capital. The Vietnam War came to an end.

This war caused terrible destruction and suffering in South East Asia. More than 1.2 million Vietnamese died in conflict. American bombing and chemical spraying caused lasting damage to farmland and forests. With the unity of Vietnam and communist regime 173000 refugees came to the USA. This war also took a heavy toll on American soldiers. About 58,000 died and more than 300,000 were wounded. Returning soldiers often had recurring nightmares and other stress related problems. Since then Americans have been less willing to get involved in overseas wars. The terroristic attacks on America in September 11, 2001 have changed public opinion. America has involved itself actively in Afghanistan and Iran to wipe out terrorism.

Landing on the Moon:

The moon has been a center of romance and affection in our folklore for all time. The 20th century dismantled our ethos about it. It proved that the moon is a ball of rock about 2,160 miles (3476 km) in diameter, nearly a quarter of the size of Earth. It does not shine by its own but rather reflects the light of the sun. The force of gravity there is much less-1/6 of the Earth. It is about 238860 miles (384400 km) away. The curiosity about the moon led man to explore space. Hence the launching of satellites in the mid-1950s was followed by the venture of the cosmonaut Yuri Gagarin, a Russian who flew into space aboard Vostok I on April 12, 1961. This was followed by the Mercury program of the USA, culminating John Glenn's three-time space flight around the Earth of February 20, 1962. It took another seven years for the next great event, the landing on the moon. On July 21, 1969 Neil Armstrong, an American, became the first person to walk on the moon. Till 1974 11 more people walked on its surface, till the program was suspended as enough samples had been collected for research. These astronauts have discovered that the surface of the moon is uneven and rocky. It is scattered with thousands of saucer shaped cavities, called craters, gouged out by falling meteorites. Its landscape is made of wide plains scarred by innumerable craters alternating with high mountains, deep crevices, and steep cliffs. The extreme old age of the lunar surface came as a big surprise. The samples have revealed that the rocks are volcanic in origin, that both the moon and the Earth are 4.6 billion years old and that there has never been any water of life on it.

Chernobyl Accident- Post War Atomic holocaust:

After the atomization of Japan in World War 2 several nations- the USSR, Britain, France, People's republic of China, India- acquired the capability of using atomic energy for war like as well as peaceful purposes. Hence hundreds of nuclear power plants came up in these countries to generate electricity etc. In Chernobyl, Russia, the biggest nuclear disaster was caused in 1986 by a combination of building defect, lack of proper maintenance and negligence on the part of technicians. This human negligence caused the explosion and blaze in the nuclear plant. A huge cloud of radioactive particles traveled towards Northeastern Europe where these particles landed. This was the worst sort of radioactive pollution mankind had ever experienced. This contaminated the plants and animals that met them. Many trees had to be cut down and the fruit and vegetables had to be thrown away to protect people from contamination. In Scandinavian countries entire herds of deer had to be destroyed. Several thousand people were affected by this pollution culminating in some 20,000 deaths. The aftereffects of this explosion are still being felt today. This had raised a huge question mark on the safety and maintenance of such plants worldwide.

Fall of Communism in Russia:

On the eve of the Bolshevik revolution in Russia in 1917, Lenin believed that communism meant a form of society in which private property had no place. The ownership of all property would be vested in the community. Labor would be organized for the common benefit of all the workers. After revolution everything was done to abolish private enterprise. USSR became the dictatorship of the Communist party. Under Stalin the USSR became a police state. The neighboring countries were swallowed one after another. Communism came to be identified with Russian imperialism. By means of communist parties in the satellite countries the Russian Presidium (Polit Bureau until 1952) controlled the governments of such countries as China, Poland, Hungary, Czechoslovakia, Bulgaria, Romania, and Albania. Communist parties in non-communist countries sought to undermine democracy in Europe, Africa, America, and Asia. Stalin died in 1953. Georgi M. Malenkov succeeded him as the head of the communist party and prime minister and Nikita Khrushchev became first secretary. In February 1955, Malenkov suddenly retired. Nikolai A. Bulganin became premier and Khrushchev head of the party. These were the days of the Cold War and the ascendency of Communism.

The USSR used its resources for armament and a 'thick curtain was extended'. In the absence of private enterprise nobody was taking a serious initiative in production. In this period revolts brew up in Hungary and Czechoslovakia. Some of the later Chinese communists freed themselves from the Russia yoke. The wind of change for democracy was blowing everywhere and the USSR was plunging into one crisis after another internally. In March 1985, when Mikhail Gorbachev became general secretary of the party, the Soviet Union was in grave economic crises which led to the collapse of the communist system. He began a restructuring (Perestroika) of soviet institutions along with 'openness' (Glasnost) in everyday life while he also improved international relations. But the communist system could survive. All East European countries- Hungary, Bulgaria, Czechoslovakia, Poland, East Germany, Romania, and Albania- left the communist system and joined the West Europe and the USA in restructuring their economies. The communists revolted against Gorbachev at home and put him under house arrest. Boris Yeltsin, the Russian leader, came to his help.

The Soviet Union was dissolved in 1991. All 16 republics on the Russian borders were freed and became separate independent countries. They regained the status they enjoyed in the 19th century. Boris Yeltsin came to power and declared himself president of Russia. He revived private enterprise and slowly the economy began to come back on track. After Yeltsin, Putin took over as president. After his tenure of ten years he became prime minister, still all powerful. Now Russia is a democratic country like others. With the help of the west the economy is improving. Still

Putin must go a long way. Now though Communism has become a history in Russia.

Terroristic Attacks on the USA:

Terrorism is a new phenomenon after the Cold War in the post-World War era. Many the countries in Europe, Asia and Africa have been facing this menace for decades for one reason or another; they may be religious, political, or extraterritorial. Groups of disgruntled elements are using terrorism as a weapon to achieve their goal notwithstanding the care for the lives of innocent people. Terrorists are using time bombs, poison, in discriminant fighting and hold ups to force the government to concede to their demands. Britain, Spain Bosnia, Croatia, Russia, India, Nepal, Indonesia, Saudi Arabia, Afghanistan, Iraq, Egypt, Sudan Zimbabwe, Kenya, Tanzania are among the sufferers. The USA had never experienced the pangs of terrorism and did not take proper note of the problem although a bomb had been exploded in the World Trade Center in New York In 1991. A few years later American embassies were bombed in Nairobi, Kenya and Darussalam, Tanzania killing hundreds of people. Several American tourists were also killed in Egypt and elsewhere around this period. Still the USA did not apply the required seriousness.

Problems of Palestine, Kashmir, Bosnia, and Chechnya took worse turns when the fanatics of the Islamic world presented them as a persecution of Muslims at the instance of the USA. Fanatic leaders like Osama Bin Laden, a South Arabian renegade, Al Jawahiri, an Egyptian demagogue, and Mulla Omer of Afghanistan who declared a jihad against America and its allies. They captured Afghanistan with the active support of Pakistan. The arms given by American to contain Russian influence were used against America. Their moral boosting victory in Afghanistan helped consolidate their position in the Islamic world. They hatched a great conspiracy. Secret preparations were made to 'teach America a lesson'. On September 11, 2001 the Americans in the world were stunned to see the most daring terroristic attack on America. One airplane belonging to American Airlines hit World Trade Tower 1, spilling 90,000 gallons of patrol inside and left the tower burning like an inferno. It was thought that some stray plane might have made a hit after mechanical failure. But after some time another airplane was seen approaching the other tower. The cameras were on and captured on the gory sight of the plane hitting and piercing into the upper stories of the Second Tower and appearing on the other side, crashing at some distance. Shockingly people learnt that it was a terrorist attack. People then saw another aircraft approaching the Pentagon in Washington DC which later destroyed some of the buildings. Brave passengers in another plane tried to cow down the terrorists. They pounced upon the terrorists and helped make the place crash in a field, killing all people on board. Both the World Trade Towers could not stand the heat generated by the burning petrol and crumbled like a building of cards. The surrounding buildings included the Solomon Tower were also badly damaged and fell. Some 5,000 workers who were inside the building were trapped and died within no time. The whole of Manhattan was in disarray. Firefighters and police came into action and tried to save lives. In doing so many of them also lost their lives. It was the shock of the new century. President Bush resolved to wipe out terrorism from the face of the Earth. It came to be known that Bin Laden and his gang was behind it and that he was in Afghanistan. The Taliban government of Afghanistan refused to extradite Bin Laden. The USA attacked Afghanistan and after heavy fighting, it was able to dislodge the Taliban. Laden is still at large. The war against terrorism is still on.

CHAPTER ELEVEN

World Wars

World War I (1914-1918):

There had been several fierce wars before this spine chilling, horrifying and devastating conflict that shook the entire world and left all countries suffering in one way or another. It is to be kept in mind that basically it was a European war and didn't have the potentials of exploding into such proportions. It was not one incident that started the war, rather the colonial aspirations of the European powers dragged the whole lot of mankind into this hell fire. Its seedlings lay in the Franco-Prussian war (1870-1871), a dispute between France and Prussia, a German state. All the other German states joined on the side of Prussia, and it became a war between France and Germany. The results were disastrous for France which was defeated at Sedan in March 1871. Germany forced France to give Alsace and Lorraine. The four German states became a united German nation under Prussian leadership. Wilhelm I was crowned as the first 'Kaiser' (emperor) of the new German empire. Otto Van Bismarck, the first Chancellor of the New Empire, used the policy of 'Iron and Blood' and nationalism in place of speeches and resolutions to expand the German empire. He tried to make it secure by forming a Triple Alliance. This guaranteed him the support of Austria-Hungary and Italy in case of aggression by Russia or France. This alliance remained in force until World War I when Italy joined the allies against Germany. Thus Bismarck had fortified Germany and imbued it with German patriotism. Although he retired in 1888, Germany continued his policy of aggrandizement.

Causes

Many nationalist movements had created an explosive situation in central Europe. The conflicts revolved around Serbia; a new state formed in 1878. Two alliances had already been formed. On one side were Britain, France, and Russia. On the other Austria-Hungary, Germany, and Italy. Many crises had preceded the war including colonial disputes in the Balkans. High tension was prevailing in Franco-German relations to the 1870-1871 war. Each great country was trying to increase its own wealth and power and there had been many clashes. Britain and France seized a sizeable and most desirable part of Africa before Germany decided to get into the colonial race. Germany tried to get a foot hold in Morocco, where France had a great influence. Britain came to France's aid, resulting in German's ambitions being checked. The Germans felt that the only hope for their country was to build a military and naval power that would challenge the strength of Britain and France. Russia and Austria both wanted to control the Balkans. Most European countries wanted a piece of the Balkan regions, which resulted in two clashes in the region.

By 1914 two groups of countries faced each other. No one knew when the war would begin. Everyone feared war and hoped to avoid it but was getting ready to fight it if necessary. No country could tell whether another was bluffing. The direct cause of war arose in Austria. For some time the country's policy had been to expand to the East to get a port on the Aegean Sea, a policy known as 'Drang nach osten" (Push forward the East). But Serbia and Montenegro were squarely across the path and Russia had promised to help protect their borders.

On July 28, 1914 the Australian crown Prince Archduke Frances Ferdinand and his wife Sophie, countess of Hohenberg, were shot at Sarajevo, the capital of the Austria province of Bosnia. The assassin was Gavrilo Prinzip, a Serb. This provided just what some of the more ambitious Austrian statesmen wanted: a reason to attack Serbia. Austria could easily defeat Serbia, and thus take another long step eastward. The Austrian government claimed that the Serbian government was responsible for the crime. Germany supported Austria in this claim. On July 23, 1914

Austria sent a stiff ultimatum to Serbia and compliance was demanded within 48 hours. The ultimatum included the expression of regret on the part of Serbia for its officer's involvement in Anti- Austrian demonstrations along with stern action against them by dismissal from services, arrest, and prosecution. It also demanded the participation of Austrian officers in judicial proceedings in Serbia against persons implicated in the Sarajevo crime. Austria would be having full authority to name them. In addition Austria wanted a declaration from the Serbian government that it would never involve itself in any Anti- Austrian activities. This declaration would be communicated by the king of Serbia to his army as an order of the day and published din the official bulletin; that all papers which had incited hatred towards Austria should be suppressed, the Nardone Odbrana (National Defense) should be dissolved and its property confiscated, elimination of any topics that incited hatred against Austria from the textbooks and that Serbia furnished Austria-Hungary with explanations of utterances of high Serbian officials who had ventured to speak ill of the Austro-Hungary government after the Sarajevo crime.

Most of the European countries believed that Serbia would not accept these demands as they told upon heavily on the sovereignty of an independent nation. But to avoid any conflict the Serbs replied promptly and accepted every demand except the involvement of Austrian officers in suppressing the movement against the integrity of the Austro-Hungarian government in Serbia and the participation of Austrian officers in their judicial proceedings. It was too much for a sovereign state to permit foreign officers to enter the country on such a mission.

Declaration of War

Austria announced that the Serbs had failed to meet the demands of the ultimatum. On July 28, 1914 Austria-Hungary declared war on Serbia. Russia at once made it clear that it considered its own interests linked with those of Serbia and the small Slav states in the Balkans. Russia mobilized its forces and declared that it would march its troops for war the day Austrian troops crossed the Serbian border. Austria chose to believe that Russians were bluffing and would not dare to attack the strong central powers. Russian attitude affected France and Britain as members of the Triple Alliance. Germany spoke in favor of localizing the dispute, which meant letting Austria-Hungary punish Serbia and take from the country what it pleased without any international interference, yet everyone knew that Germany would support its ally. Italy announced its neutrality. The Russian mobilization was a direct threat to the Austro-Hungarian Empire. In support of its ally Austria, Germany declared war on Russia on August 1, 1914.

At the beginning of the war the world was amazed to see the German preparations to strike a mighty blow. The German emperor, in command of the most powerful army the world had ever seen, became the dominant army in Europe. The German general staff planned to overwhelm France within a month or less, turn sharply and defeat Russia in the east. With these two powers reduced it would then turn its attention to Britain which was not expected to offer much resistance. In the south whatever resistance the Balkan states offered was to be speedily overcome and a clear road was to be opened into Asia. As soon as it was clear that war was imminent France moved 200,000 men towards the eastern frontier. These forces took position six miles from the border, below the Belgian and Luxemburg borders.

War begins

The German chiefs asked Belgium for freedom to pass through the kingdom as it was the easiest route to France. The German government promised full payment after the war for damage which might done to Belgian property in the peaceful passage. The Belgian king Albert declared "Belgium is a nation, not a road". His government refused the German demand for free passage through Belgium into France. As a result, on August 4, German armies where hurled upon Belgian soil. This brought Britain into the war. The same day Britain declared war on Germany. A day earlier Germany had done so in relation to France. It was a chain reaction and by the end of August, ten nations had declared their participation in the war, including Japan which was taking the side of Britain, France, and Russia.

The First Battle of Mern

German troops were marching through Belgium driving back the French, Belgians and British. On September 5, 1914 the allied armies, under Marshall Joseph Jacques and General Joseph Gallienne checked the attack of Germany general Alexander Von Klauck at the Mern River. On September 6 the actual battle began. On September 8 the Germans began to retreat and did not stop until they reach the Aisne River. France was safe for the time being. The Germans had grabbed 1/10 of its territory. Antwerp camp of Belgians was besieged by German forces under General

Eric Von Falkenhayn who planned to occupy the channel ports. On October 10 the Belgians surrendered in the face of heavy artillery fire from the Germans. The loss of Antwerp was a great blow but the German plans to advance down the coast ran haywire by the delay.

British Reverses

The main British force was transferred from the Aisne to the new left of the allied line. In a heroic defense at Ypres, Belgium, the British regular army was almost wiped out. Britain now began the long task of building a new fighting force. By the end of the year nearly 1,000,000 men had enlisted, and the British Empire had altogether 2,000,000 under arms. Even a year after the battle of Mern, however, the British army was poorly prepared to take its place on the side of France on the battlefield

Battle fronts

The line on the Western Front extended for 450 miles from the English Channel to Switzerland and held the closest attention of the world. Second in interest but greatest in length, the Eastern Front was the line along the Eastern Boundaries of the Central Empires. It stretched from Riga on the Baltic Sea to the shores of the Black sea, 1,125 miles. When Italy entered the war on 1915 another front was established. It ran from Switzerland along the Italian frontiers almost to Trieste and was about 320 miles long. Before the war ended another line was established through the southern Balkan regions. This line was about 300 miles long. In most places both sides dug trenches to protect themselves. A new kind of war developed in which swift movements and pitched battles had no part. Months after months entrenched armies held their positions hoping to wear out the enemy. Only main points were fortified but it took an army of half a million men.

1915

The Western Front settled down and remained almost unchanged for two years. British and France took advantage of the chance to build munitions plants. The actual fighting took the form of artillery warfare and few movements back and forth by both sides. Some fierce battles were fought around Verdun. In April 1915 the Germans began a strong movement to capture the French city of Calais on the English Channel. Using poison gas, never used in war, they gained three miles. Two German attacks on Ypres were turned by, largely by the heroism of Canadian regiments. All through the summer of 1915 bitter fighting continued from the trenches. Western Belgium and north eastern France were a maze of trenches on a line of 12 miles. The most important allied gain was the capture of a vast German underground fortress of steel and concrete known as 'The Labyrinth'. In September the British and French began tremendous drive in the French district of Champagne and Artois and in Belgium. The Germans were driven back three miles, but the allies could not break through. At the end of the year the allies had only won back 50 square miles of territory from invaders.

Eastern Front

The Germans expected the Russians to attack through Poland in the direction of Berlin. The German forces could easily strike from the North or south and cut off Russia's finest army. Grand Duke Nicholas, the commander of the Russian army, first attacked farther north in East Prussia, and far to the south, in Galicia. Bon Hindenburg defeated the Russians in the north, gaining success in Masuria lake regions. But in the South the Russian armies were at first successful. The advance against the Austrians took the important city of Lemberg on September 3, 1914 and after a seven-month siege captured Pizamysl on March 22, 1915.

Hindenburg attacked Poland. He was within seven miles of Warsaw in October 14 when Nicholas turned him back. The Austrians were decimated in the Carpathian snows and Krakow was threatened. The victorious Russian army carried on and Von Mackanin's Germans, by a marvelous feat at arms, nearly wiped them out. Hindenburg once again struck towards Warsaw and was once again checked by Nicholas. Both sides dug in, their positions unchanging till the middle of 1915

The Austrians, with great numbers of fresh troops, tried to attack the Russians in Galicia but were badly defeated. The Russians seized all the important Carpathian passes and held them until June 1915. At the end of 1914, Germany and Austria-Hungary were on the defensive among most of the Eastern front.

In 1915 the Russians began to run out of munitions. The Central power massed powerful forces all along the line and gained much territory. Russia was driven out of Galicia and lost Lemberg. Warsaw surrendered in early

August. In September the Central powers captured Vilma and threatened Riga. The Czar himself took command on the Eastern front.

The Dardanelles Campaign

In Januarys 1915 the Russian high command appealed to Great Britain for an attack which would relieve the pressure on Russia's army in the Caucasus. Instead the British decided upon a naval expedition upon the Dardanelles to take the Gallipoli peninsula and Constantinople. After a bombardment of the Turkish ports, the fleet entered the straits on March 18. In the face of casualties the attempt was abandoned. Then they tried to land British, French, Australian and New Zealand troops on the peninsula. They were successful but heavy enemy firing forced them to withdraw. The failure had a far-reaching effect. It not only left Constantinople in Turkish possession but also lowered ally prestige throughout the Balkan countries.

Serbia Overwhelmed

Austria-Hungary overran Serbia and captured Belle grad on December 2, 1914. After two weeks in a strong counterattack, Serbia regained its capital. In June 1915 Bulgaria entered the war on the side of the central powers. Foreseeing a chance to get back the land lost during the early Balkan war. By December regrouped German Austrian and Bulgarian forces overwhelmed Serbia again.

The Salonika Fiasco

In October 1915 Britain and France had sent troops from Gallipoli to Salonika after realizing threat to Serbia. At the Serbian frontier this force found itself cut off by Bulgarians and fell back to Salonika, where it remained until 1914. Fresh divisions of allied troops were sent to Salonika and there the defeated Serbian army was reassembled. Although half a million in number, they could not achieve anything worth mention. To all intent and purpose they were interned at Salonika. Yet the allies dared not withdraw them, for fear of losing prestige.

1916: in the west

Before the end of 1915, the central powers made a bid for peace based on
"the map of Europe". This meant they should keep what they have taken. The allies turned down this proposal. The greatest event of 1916 was the battle of Verdun, the central gateway to Paris. The German crowned prince commanded the army which began the assault. The battle continued from February 21 until near the early part of September. Finally Germans gave up the plan in face of stiff opposition. During this period the allies were preparing for a great offensive farther north, along the Somme River. There great guns destroyed miles of trench works of steel and concrete. Military tanks were first used in an attack the allies made on Courcelette. Day after day until December the allies steadily pushed back the Germans in the east. On this front Russia had taken advantage of the winter months to organize more thoroughly and to gather great stores of munitions. Before winter Russia had overrun the crown land of Bucovina and again threatened Lemberg. The Austrians were driven back into the Carpathian Mountains.

Summersault of Italy

On May 3, 1915 Italy denounced the triple alliance and on May 23 declared war on Austria. For two months small battles were fought on many parts of the 320-mile front. In August 1916 Italy made important advances along the Isonzo River and plateau. The high point of the years was the capture of Gorizia.

Romania crushed

Romania joined the allies in August 1916. Immediately after war was declared the Russian army invaded Transylvania. They seized and strengthened mountain passes in the Carpathians. Austria-Hungary was in no position to fight them because of its severe defeats by the Russians. Germany and Bulgaria therefore were assigned to punish Romania. There army swept to the Black sea. They captured Bucharest in December and seized about half of Romania, with rich resources of oil and wheat.

On other fronts

In Romania Grand duke Nicholas conducted a successful Russian campaign capturing Erzurum, Trebizond, Essington and Bayburt. Turkey made several attempts to cross the Syrian Desert and strike at the Suez Canal but the British drove them back. The situation in Greece was precarious. Serbian forces driven out of their homeland took refuge on the Grecian islands and then head to be transferred to Salonika. Until now Greece had shown a neutral face. However weak patriots favored the allies and were fighting against Bulgaria. The allies doubted the intentions of King Constantine as he was the brother in law of the German Kaiser. Therefore as a measure of precaution they blockaded the Greek coast.

New weapons: Tanks

A new engine of war known as the Tank appeared in 1916. The first tank, made in the United States, was a modified form of the Holt Caterpillar tractor. The motor of the tank was enclosed in heavy armor with small holes for sighting and for machine guns. The terrorized the enemy. After the first surprise however Central Powers learned to offset their effectiveness by heavy gunfire and began to build their own tanks. The tanks increased the potentiality of damage in the war.

1917

The year opened with hope for the allies as their great resources were beginning to make themselves felt. Germany also had reasons for hope as its armies held vast territories of the allies. The German submarine campaign was frightening. Neutral shippers stayed out of the war zones for weeks. One of four British ships that left these ports never returned. It seemed quite possible that the submarines might starve Britain into surrendering.

USA enters the War

The USA had been neutral throughout the early part of the war. Manufacturers of war material in America wanted to sell their armaments to both warring factions. Since Britain controllable the seas it was easy to make sure that American goods could go only to allies. Moreover the allies were ready to buy everything. Germany saw the USA as a storehouse of materials for the allies. Using submarines the Germans tried to cut off the flow of supplies to the allied countries. Many American ships were sunk, and American lives and property lost. On April 26, 1917 The USA declared war on Germany. During the year Pope Benedict 15 made some efforts for peace. He sent a note to each of the warring powers. From the Allies side USA president Woodrow Wilson made it clear that the allies could not make peace with a government it could not trust.

In the west

The Great battle of Verdun ended in 1916. Nothing was accomplished by either side until 1917 when the French attacked on both sides of the Meuse River and took territory along a front of 11 miles. They won back in three days what the crown prince's army had taken from them in six months. The important military operation took place in the northeastern part of France and Belgium. The combined allied forces made an offensive that threatened to destroy German morale in that section. In June the British exploded a series of mines on a ten-mile front at Messines, Belgium. This feat and operation which followed during the next few days drove the Germans back three miles along a five-mile front.

Late in November, British major general Sir Julian Byung planned and carried out a surprise attack against Cambria, France. Over a front of 30 miles Germans under the crown prince Ruprecht were pushed back more than five miles and driven to a desperate defense of Cambria, with the British only two miles away. Byung lost almost all his gains to a German counterattack.

Russia drops out

On March 15 Russians overthrew their government and forced the Czar to abdicate. He was imprisoned. They declared to the world that Russia was free from monarchy. The allied hailed this revolution with joy, for the czar's desire for peace was well known and the revolutionaries had announced that they would carry forward war efforts. The Russian armies drove the Austrian armies back in Galicia and threatened them in Poland. Russia was in no position to go on fighting, however. The Russian armies were short of equipment, hungry, war weary and could not be held in line. Fighters laid down their arms in dozens of brigades. Then in September a German army and over half the navy made a demonstration in the direction in the Gulf of Finland. On the way they captured Riga, a great seaport, without resistance. Pressing onwards they took Ousel and Dago islands. The way was opened to the fort at Ronstadt and to the Russian capital Petrograd (now Leningrad). Just then the provisional government was overthrown by a council of workingmen and soldiers in November. The Communists seized power. In this bloody coup 10,000 people were killed. Leaders of this revolution were Nikolai Lenin and Leon Trotsky, who was made foreign minister. The New regime announced to make peace with the Central Powers. On December 8, the new government brought hostilities to an end. But the Germans demanded for themselves all occupied territory. Trotsky refused to make peace, but he also declared they would not declare war. Persuasion by the US president Woodrow Wilson also failed to inspire Russia. The situation was so bad that on March 3, Trotsky signed the humiliating peace treaty Brest-Litovsk. Germany was given Livonia, Estonia, Courtland and the Allan Islands and its title to Poland was confirmed.

Italian reverses

Being freed from the Russian front Germans rushed to help Austria-Hungary at Vaporetto. Within three days they won 1,000 sq miles of territory from Italy. The Italian army retreated to the Pave River. At this stage, alarmed with developments, England and France hastened to Italy's aid. Before December heavy reinforcements arrived from the Western front and the attack was stopped.

The war in Asia

Near the end of 1915 an Anglo-Indian expeditionary force appeared north of the Persian Gulf. Its objective was Baghdad. In November the British successfully attacked the Turks south of Baghdad. In December they were defeated and were driven to Kut-Al-Amara. On April 29, 1916 the British force of 10,000 men and officers surrendered because of threatened starvation. Another force, which had tried to relieve the first, captured Baghdad in March 1917 and pushed on north of the city. The British army in Asia continued its task of lessening the territory and the influence of the Central Powers in the Sultan's territory. By December 1917 it had fought its way to within three miles of Jerusalem and on December 9 the captured it.

1918

The great German offensive on the western front began on March 21, 1918 in Picardy within the Oise and Scarpe rivers. After fierce fighting the allied army retreated slowly for 10 days. By April 6, the great attack had been stopped in the face of the United Allied Command under French general Foch. On April 9, the offensive was underway once more. This time the Germans struck to the north in the Armentieres section south of Ypres but gained only about 17 miles.

The Battle for Paris

On May 17, the battle began again. The most active section was the line from the Chemin des Dams through Noyon to Cantigny and northward to Arras. The allied army was pushed back. Another offensive was launched in the region of Ypres in a new effort to reach the channel ports. The outlook for the allies was discouraging. Their newspapers were preparing their readers for the fall of Paris. The victorious Germans turned their best battalions in the direction of Paris. They reached the bank of the Merna River on May 31. At Belleauwood 6,000 of 8,000 American marines were killed. But the line held. The American reinforcement attacked the Germans but was pushed back. In a successful counterattack thought Chateau Thierry was cleared of Germans on July 2. Paris was saved. From now onwards the Germans were on the defensive. The steady increase in the number of American troops gave Foch superiority in numbers. Then he began a series of hammering blows to Germans on the entire 200-mile line. The German line began to fall back. By August 18, the allied lines ran south by east from Albert to Soissons. Meanwhile the allied forces near the North Sea exerted such pressure that Belgian soil was recovered mile by mile.

The last days

By August the Americans were holding 39 miles of the French front. The Great success had been achieved by pushing ahead along the shoreline and pinching the Germans into small pockets from which they had to retreat to avoid surrender. In the north the enveloping campaigns was extending into Belgium. The allied were driving the Germans south and east, giving them no rest.

On September 12, more than 700,000 Americans attacked the Germans at Saint Michael. The French units were on the flanks. In two days the enemy had been pushed back from this triangular area and the fighting line ran almost directly southeast from Verdun to within two miles of the Lorraine border. Then the grinding campaign began north of Verdun, in the region of Argonne Forest along the Muse River. By October 15 the great naval guns of the United States mounted on railroad cars were throwing shells upon the forts around Metz, twelve miles away.

Germany's collapse

The German army had been retreating since July. The news of the situation was reaching beyond the Rhine and the German people began to understand that they had been deceived. Bulgaria had surrendered, Austria-Hungary was wavering, Turkey had given up and Germany practically stood alone.

The Kaiser placed Prince Maximilian of Baden in the post of Imperial Chancellor on October 3 and gave him the task of seeking an armistice. Socialists were admitted to the ministry. Within a few days they had control of the government and President Wilson was informed that the government of the people was ready to discuss peace. The emperor left Berlin and sought refuge with his army. The Chancellor demanded that the Kaiser abdicate. Von Hindenburg agreed. William II therefore had to agree. In the early morning of November 10 he entered the Netherlands to seek safety from his own soldiers.

In the meantime Marshall Foch had given German government his armistice terms and 72 hours to surrender. The Germans accepted the terms at 11 AM November 11, 1918. The fighting ceased and the war was over.

By the terms of the armistice, over 70 German Vessels of all classes- from mighty battleships to submarines and destroyers- were delivered to the allies in December 1918. The British naval forces took possessions of German overseas colonies early in the war. Allies occupied Togoland in Africa, the only self-supporting German colony. There they captured the Cameroons in 1915. General Botha of South Africa conquered West Africa (Namibia) in 1916 and German East Africa, the largest and richest of the German colonies, was taken in 1918. This included Tanganyika and Uganda. Airplanes were used for the first time in this war. In the beginning they could fly only 90 miles per hour and carry only two people. In 1917 they were carrying two people along with a ton of bombs and machine guns at the speed of 175 miles per hour. Despite these developments' airpower played little importance in the war.

The terms of this armistice left Germany dismembered, disarmed and under constant guard. Payment for damages done by its forces in invaded territories, the return of cash taken from the national bank of Belgium and the return of gold taken from Russia and Romania was enforced on the vanquished nation.

Treaty of Versailles

The Treaty of Versailles officially ending the war was signed on June 28, 1919 in the Hall of Mirrors of the palace of Versailles. USA played an important part in drawing it up. The Big Three- President Woodrow Wilson of the USA, and Premiers Lloyd George of Great Britain and Georges Clemenceau of France- expressed great satisfaction. According to the treaty there were four outstanding provisions, 43 revisions of boundaries, the setting of reparations, the disarming of Germany and the establishment of the League of Nations.

Germany lost the provinces of Alsace and Lorraine, much of Schleswig, the districts of Eupen, Malmedy, southeastern Silesia, Posen and a strip with Prussia which was granted to Poland as a corridor to the sea. The Mouth of Memel and the surrounding territory was seceded to the allies and later transferred to Lithuania. The city of Denzing was taken from Germany and made into a free city under the jurisdiction of the League of Nations. Germany lost all its overseas colonies and its rights in Turkey and China. The Rhineland was demilitarized. It was to be occupied for a term of years to assure Germany's good behavior.

Germany had to turn over to the allies' livestock for the farms the German armies had laid waste, ships, railroad cars, locomotives and other materials to replace those destroyed during the war and a large quantity of coal to repay France for the losses in its own mines in addition to the payments of large yearly sums. The reparations were finally set by a commission in 1921 at 132,000,000,000 Gold Marks, or about $33,000,000,000. Germany never paid these reparations.

Surprisingly the USA did not ratify the treaty. Although after much deliberations Germany ratified, its scar ran deep into the Germans side and later gave Hitler a chance to raise Germany's power once again. It filled the Germans with the feeling of hatred towards Britain and France.

Cost of the War

There were about 320,000,000 casualties including a death toll of 8,000,000 soldiers. Russia alone had 8765000 casualties followed by 6325000 of Germany. The war cost the nations that took part about $200,000,000,000. Its results were so dreadful that many people hoped mankind had learned a lesson. Winners, losers, and onlookers alike suffered so terribly that it was hard to believe the countries of the world would ever take up arms. The war did not settle that problems that had caused it though. Therefore at the most, the 20 years peace (1919-1939) provided time for a new buildup to bring the ugly and horrifying face of the war with new vengeance. The short-lived memory of mankind forgot the holocaust of the war.

World War II (1939-1945):

During the 6,000-year-old human civilization the world never faced a greater Holocaust than the Second World War during 1939-1945. This war stretched to four out of seven continents and engulfed all races, cultures, and cream of youth throughout the world. The first World War (1914-1918) was thought to be the bloodiest conflict in which ten million men had died in trenches and killing fields of Europe. Another 20 million were wounded. After the end of the war humans hopes that a new world order would prevent the outbreak of more terrible conflicts. But its seeds remained inherent in the peace plant.

The Treaty of Versailles signed in the summer of 1919, required Germany to give up its colonies and drastically reduce the size of its army and navy, confess the responsibility to start war and pay the damages to the allies. It left the German people feeling humiliated. Foreseeing the ramifications of this treaty, Marshall Ferdinand Foch, an allied commander, prophetically said, "This is not peace. It's an armistice for twenty years"

Stroke of time shattered the dreams of peace as its greatest epitome Woodrow Wilson, the US president, was forced by his countrymen not to go ahead in any further European mess. Consequently the USA refused to guarantee the borders of France, ratify the Treaty of Versailles, and join the League of Nations. A step further: the USA army that had only recently defeated the Germans was quickly dismantled. Britain and France had lost the cream of its youth. Russia was suffering through a revolution followed by a civil war; it was denied any participation in the post war global order. With the death of Wilson and Lenin in 1924 the dream of world peace was virtually over.

Mussolini had come to power In Italy and was nursing a dream to raise the Roman Empire once again. In Germany a charismatic war hero, Adolf Hitler, mobilized the middle class against communism, the Treaty of Versailles, and the Jews. He thundered that 'the Third Reich must avenge Germany's defeat and dominate Europe, perhaps even the world'.

This self-proclaimed 'Fuhrer' (leader) marched from rally to rally (Hitler over Germany). Taken in by his terrific oratory the Media also promoted him. As a result, by 1929, more than 100,000 Germans had joined the Nazi party of Hitler. At the same time German industrialists, alarmed at their country's deterioration started to support him. To add fuel to the fire the Depression laid havoc with the economy of Europe and America. All suffered from curtailed production and staggering unemployment. It was prelude to political catastrophe. In Germany, with five million or more unemployed, Adolf Hitler seized power and became chancellor in 1933. Since there was no order in Europe he declared "only domination or submission". Franklin D. Roosevelt, the newly elected President of the USA, was concentrating on the Depression; hence he treated Europe as a secondary problem. At that time the USA was maintaining an army smaller than that of Poland. Engrossed with her own economic problems, the US did not wish to be drawn into a new European war and passed a series of neutrality acts.

Britain and France were the reluctant guarantors of the peace treaty they had created. French Premier Eduard Daladier and British Prime Minister Neville Chamberlin along with their statesmen feared that a new war would lead to another massacre of their young generation as well as communist expansion. Thus they felt compelled to appease Hitler and Mussolini.

Fearing no retribution the Nazi robbed and persecuted Jews, began to raise a modern air force and enlarge their army. In 1935 Mussolini invaded and later conquered Ethiopia, a member of the League of Nations. None intervened against him. Ethiopian emperor Haile Selassie went before the League in Geneva to issue an appeal for help. European leaders connived at the doings of Mussolini as they later would to Hitler. This was practically the end of the League of Nations. In 1938 Hitler annexed Austria and threatened to dismember the Czech Republic. Chamberlin flew to Munich, conferred with Hitler, accepted his dismemberment of Czechoslovakia, and returned home proclaiming "Peace in our times". But to Hitler it was the death warrant of the old man and he was to fill in the date. In Spain Hitler and Mussolini helped General Francisco Franco lead an uprising against the freely elected government. The democracies did little for the other side and Franco won. Once again aggression fed upon democratic indecision. Hitler began to formulate new demands this time against Poland. Alarmed with these demands Britain and France began to rearm. Voices of dissent against Chamberlin's policy of appeasing were becoming louder and clear and Churchill was gaining a broader audience. Franklin Roosevelt in the USA took notice of Hitler's designs, but it was impossible to push a recalcitrant public towards rearmament. Meanwhile Hitler thundered that he had freed Germany from the 'death sentence of Versailles'. He had created a greater Germany and enlisted Mussolini as a second fiddle and threatened further expansion by preparing to attack Poland. Stunned at these developments Britain and France turned to Stalin, hoping for his support in defense of Poland. Now it was Stalin's turn to show his distrust for Britain and France. Moreover he also had expansionist plans. He and Hitler entered into a secret agreement to divide Poland and much of Eastern Europe between them.

War's start

On September 1, 1939 Hitler invaded Poland from the west. Two days later, on September 3, Britain and France declared war on German. The die for World War II had been cast. The Western powers watched the fall of Poland helplessly. Soon Hitler's plans for a 'Blitzkrieg' (lightning warfare) threatened to overrun France and the Low Countries appeared to be taking shape.

In the Far East

Hitler had developed close ties with Japan, also showing signs of aggression. By 1939 Japan had plundered much of China. The USA was shocked by Japanese brutality in that country and suspended trade with Japan. Gloom surrounded the West. At this time President Roosevelt took a bold decision and was soon working to ship arms and ammunitions to Britain and France. Still the future looked grim for the west. Churchill wrote "The English-speaking people through unwisdom, carelessness and good nature allowed the wicked to rearm".

On the Chinese front, Japan's well trained and equipped infantry devoured one city after another. Despite barbed wire and artillery fire the Japanese army charged into Beijing. Short of everything but manpower and largely ignored by the West, China desperately signed a nonaggression pact with the Soviet Union, which secretly agreed to supply weapons to this much harried ally.

Spain

Spain's civil war lasted for 33 months but killed 600,000 and by 1939 General Franco was well entrenched in the seat of power. An estimated 500,000 refugees crossed over into France. But London and Paris recognized Franco as the ruler of Spain, a position he held for 36 years. Germany had helped Franco, but he politely refused to join the axis powers- Germany, Italy, and Japan. During this period there was worldwide propaganda against the Jews, who were being hounded in almost all of Europe.

Finland

A nonaggression pact with the Nazis in the summer of 1939 allowed the Soviet Union to absorb its Baltic neighbors within the year. When it attacked Finland in November, a real but one-sided war broke out when the Soviets attacked. The Fins slipped away, and then counterattacked. But civilians were bombed and in March 1940 Finland surrendered. Soviets won after a heavy loss of life.

1940

The year in 1940 presented Western Civilization with an unprecedented catastrophe. This was the fall of France. Such a thing had not happened even during the bloody years of World War I.

After the destruction of Poland, there was lull and no attack in the West had materialized. The spin-doctor of allies had a false believe that their propaganda had forced Hitler to develop cold feet and reconsider. These conceited people believed that the much-vaunted Maginot Line which had consumed so many billions in French defense funds would keep the dirty Fuhrer at bay while France and Britain built up their strength. Simultaneously Hitler and his generals evolved the brilliant Manstein Plan, aimed at striking at the Achilles heel in France's defense, where the Maginot Line was incomplete. Notwithstanding the British naval supremacy, Hitler marched northward into Denmark and crossed the Baltic into Norway. It was clear that the long-awaited offensive in the West could not be far off. Denmark fell in a day with hardly in a shot fired. On the same day Germany invaded, it landed troops in Norway. For the first time parachutists were deployed in an airborne assault. Hitler wanted the air and naval bases in Norway and Swedish iron ore export shipped through the northern port of Narvia. German scientists coveted

Norway's ability to produce 'heavy water' essential for the development of nuclear weapons. With little resistance, Oslo surrendered. King Haakon VII fled to London with Norwegian gold reserves worth millions, but not before sinking 10 German destroyers in a major battle. Of course the British Navy was responsible for it. After Denmark and Norway it was Belgium's turn. On May 10 Hitler restarted the airborne attack and ferocious armored assault. Though its army fought bravely it was no match for well-equipped Germans. Neutral Holland was capitulated on the 14th. The fall of Belgium's Fort Eben Emael, said to be the world's strongest and lynchpin of Belgian defense, was France's real bad news. Even before negotiations for surrender on May 14, The Luftwaffe (German air force) bomber the center of Rotterdam, Holland's biggest port, killing 800 people and wounding several thousand. It was Hitler's way to force his enemies to surrender. Queen Wilhelmina escaped to England and set up a government in exhale. Resistance continued throughout the war.

Fall of France

The French army 97 divisions strong, was powerful at least on paper. It had more tanks than the Germans and some that were indeed better, but it had no conception of massing them in the way the Germans had demonstrated in Poland. They were shattered out thinly and ineffectively. By May 13 the Panzers- seven armored divisions strong- had burst through the supposedly impassable Ardennes Forest, on the Belgian frontier and across the Muse River at the French city of Sedan. Not covered by the Maginot line, the sector was held by only two second grade divisions of reservists. The Panzers moved into the open country of Eastern France. Premier Paul Reynard admitted before Churchill that the battle was lost. Though the Germans were not little more than hundred miles from Paris, outside government circles the citizens lived life as usual. Suddenly the picture changed with the tide of refugees from Belgium. On May 20 the Germans reached the English Chanel near Abbeville. They had effectively split the allied forces and trapped the British Expeditionary Force and French armies in the north in a deadly pocket with the backs to the sea. The BEF commanding general, Lord Girt, now concentrated on evacuation from Denmark. Here Hitler committed a blunder by issuing halt orders to his advancing army. The miracle of Dunkirk came to pass; 338,000 men including 110000 French were evacuated by the Royal army. Had Hitler not issued those orders the fate of the cornered 338,000 soldiers would have been sealed and both France and Britain would be doomed. These errors gave Britain a chance to breath and face the challenge for the next three years. After Dunkirk the German campaign became largely a matter of marching. Paris was declared an open city and on June 22 France was forced to agree to a humiliating armistice.

Even during this period French forces lost 100,000 men in six weeks to Germany's 27,074. The battle had long been lost in advance. France, internally demoralized, her generals out of date and too political minded; Britain unprepared and for Germany Manstein Plan for which the Panzers marched into an almost perfect military blueprint for victory. Like Napoleon's Austerlitz in 1805, it was Hitler's most brilliant campaign. One flaw lay in not subsequently defeating Britain and that to send Hitler, like Napoleon, to his ultimate doom in Russia.

In Britain, Churchill had taken the seat of power from Chamberlin and with his bulldog determination he was ready to fight to the finish. He was joined by the French brigadier General Charles De Gaulle, a man of equal guts. Around him he collected his tiny troop of free French who refused to submit.

Surprisingly Hitler failed to bring Operation Sea lion in August; there would be no invasion of Britain. Instead he would force Britain to saturation bombing on London and other cities. With the fall of France and bombing blitz on England it was now clear that the struggle could only by fought with Soviet and American involvement.

The bombing killed more than 43,000 British civilians and injured nearly 51,000 from July 1940 to May 1941. Yet the embattled island's will to prevail grew stronger as the attacks continued. The subway stations sheltered as many as 177,000 citizens at night and 1.5 million women and children were evacuated from London to escape night bombing.

Italy invaded Greece through Albania and conquered it in October. For two weeks the campaign went well then came into a light Greek infantry familiar with mountain terrain. The battalion retreated into Albania. Italy was shocked to learn that the British navy had sunk three of its battleships at Taranto. Still officially neutral the US began tilting its heart towards its desperate allies and beefing up its own military. After winning the third term Franklin Roosevelt developed his Lend-Lease policy, a crucial lifeline that began with antiquated weapons and eventually totaled some $50 million in arms. Churchill called this program 'Hitler's death warrant'.

1941

In World War II British and French empires were involved right from September 1939 but it assumed global dimensions of unprecedented scope and ferocity only in 1941. There was naval action on all oceans and fighting in the African continent, Eastern Asia and around Australia, preparations for the attack on the Soviet Union and war on the USA.

Simultaneously the Japanese government to take advantage of the defeat of France and the Netherlands and the lightly defeat of Britain by seizing the Pacific Asian colonies and American possessions as well. The first step was taken by occupying northern French Indochina in September. Mussolini's rule in Italy was being threatened in the face of defeat in Libya. To avoid the collapse, Hitler sent General Erwin Rommel to help the Italian force hold remnants of Italy's colonial empire. Germany needed Romania's oil and occupied it. Berlin wanted to preclude a Balkan front that could disrupt their operations while attacking the Soviet Union. The occupation of Greece and Yugoslavia was necessary. Therefore they included them in the Balkan campaign of 1941. Without much difficulty these countries were crushed. Crete was captured by airborne attack. The Greeks inflicted heavy losses on the Germans. Excess forces rushed in from Romania and Bulgaria. The Greeks, encouraged by 58,000 soldiers, fought bravely but by late 1941 the Nazi flag was flying atop the Acropolis. British soldiers fled to the coast for evacuation. In Yugoslavia occupiers hanged ten citizens to one German killed or wounded in Gancedo. The Serbs were happy at German aggression and welcomed them as liberators. They declared independence from Yugoslavia and Germans established a fascist puppet state. They harassed and murdered Serbs, Jews, and Gypsies. Hoping to replace British influence in Iraq with axis control, some pro German nationalists tried to push out the British. This failed in spite German assistance made possible by the Vicky French authorities in Syria and lead to the invasion of the country by British forces. On June 22, the day after the Syrian capital of Damascus was taken by Britain, Germany and its allies in Europe attacked the Soviet Union. Stalin had tried to avert war with Germany and rather help it with supplies and a naval base. It hoped to join the tripartite pact "Germany, Italy and Japan"

Germans had a definite plan for the invasion of the Soviet of Union. It implied that the Soviet state would collapse after initial defeats and that the campaign would be over before the winter set in. The occupation of the Soviet Union would provide Germany with two things: vast space to settle German farmers and the raw materials, such as oil, for war. Major Russian cities would be razed to the ground and their population of 40 million would starve to death as their military appropriated food. This quick victory would be followed by the conquest of the Middle East and Northwest Africa. The Germans did indeed win initial victories. The Soviet regime however was able to maintain its hold on the unoccupied territory, as Alexander I had done when Napoleon's army had reached Moscow in the early 19th century. As the season changed, 'General winter' took its toll and the story of the Napoleonic army was repeated.

From June 1941 most of the fighting in World War II took place in the eastern front but at the same time the other program of mass slaughter-the most shameful deed in the history of mankind- began in the form of wiping out the Jewish community. It started in the occupied territory of the Soviet Union and quickly expanded to all of Europe that was in the German's reach. In this holocaust, according to rough estimates, some six million Jews were slaughtered. The Nazis took mass slaughter to horrific new levels with specialized killing equipment's.

Germany attacked the Soviet Union on June 22, revoking without warning their non-aggression pact. The Soviet Union, with its communist government and large Jewish population, represented everything that Hitler hated. A few days before Stalin had disbanded the army of its most seasoned officers and ignored the warning of an impending attack. Therefore it thought to be a ripe target. Nazi troops advanced rapidly through small border towns. Taken aback the Soviet forces reeled back. Stalin described it as "the perfidious military act on our fatherland" and exhorted Soviet citizens of every faith and ethnic background to face the enemy with full might. The citizens responded by forgetting all misdeeds of the communists and rallied behind Stalin. Germans reached Leningrad in September and laid siege for 900 days. The population began dying from air raids, artillery, hunger and cold. One million became the horrific toll. Finally in early 1943 when the Soviets opened a corridor to the city at the cost of 250,000 soldier casualties, Leningrad took its proud place in the history of World War II.

German forces were closing in on Moscow by the start of December. They were only 10 miles away. Earlier, more than 100,000 citizens, especially women, had been recruited to dig tank traps outside the city limits. They did their work in perfection. Every able-bodied man between the age of 16 and 50 had been drafted into the military. Fortunately for the Soviet Union the winter of 1941 was both early and fierce, hitting subzero temperatures before the holidays. The overconfident Germans had hoped to be in the Red Square much earlier. Hence, they were wearing summer uniforms and boots. The Red army was quick to exploit the weather; encircled soldiers were able to fight their way out of a blizzard. The Nazis floundered as their weapons would not work in the cold; they suffered horribly from frostbite. 2,000 soldiers would require amputation. Their supplies dwindled. Roads were often impassable. The German offensive collapsed on December 5. The next day the Soviets, with battle planes in the sky and British tanks on the ground, counterattacked. German casualties soared past a million. The USA President FDR had already extended 'Lend-lease' to the Soviet Union. Like Napoleon, Hitler had committed a blunder by attacking the Soviet Union; a horrifying defeat was hovering around him.

Pearl Harbor

Japan on the eastern front had also decided to take control of the Pacific by attacking the Hawaii islands. Its most powerful aircraft 'the Akagi', along with 20 other vessels, was steaming secretly towards Hawaii. The Japanese rationale for war was it had to import 80% of its oil. The US had cut off exports and had demanded Japan to leave from its conquered territories that supplied much of the rest. Tokyo considered it an economic blackmail. Hence a military response, it's only choice. The strike force was within 160 miles of Honolulu, hidden by storm front, and maintained strict radio silence to remain undetected. The carriers turned into the wind for launching the first of its 360 bombers and fighters. At 6 AM that Sunday of the 7th December, pilots and air crews hurried across the flight deck of the Shokaku to their planes. A few minutes later the order to launch aircrafts was given and the carrier crew watched the attack that would change history. It had been carefully planned for months and executed with precision. US intelligence had failed. The Japanese had purposely timed their raid for Sunday morning, when the US warships and anti-aircraft guns would be undermanned. Their planes were spotted on the army radar at 7AM but ignored. Less than two hours later the pacific battle fleet was in ruins. Battleships were special targets: the 'Arizona', the 'West Virginia' and the 'Tennessee' were badly damaged. In all 18 ships were sunk that day. Two US aircraft carriers escaped doom. There were 4,575 military casualties at Pearl Harbor including 2,403 killed. 188 US planes were destroyed on the ground. It was a great shock to the USA, which had to now enter the war to salvage her prestige. Like the Germans planned to attack the Soviet Union, Japan's decision to attack Pearl Harbor was a great folly and proved counterproductive. It brought certain doom to the Axis powers. This was the turning of the war. On December 8 President Roosevelt signed the declaration of war and helped lead America and the world to victory.

1942

The New Year opened with the military disaster in the Pacific. The Japanese were in full control of the air and sea lanes that enabled their armies to advance speedily in Malaysia, Burma, and Philippians. By mid-February Singapore, the Gibraltar of the east, surrendered to the Japanese army. By May the British and Chinese army had been driven out of Burma. In the Philippians too, the US soldiers surrendered, and the island fortress of Corregidor fell on May 6. In the Dutch East Indies, the Japanese navy inflicted a crushing defeat on the combined Dutch, US, and British forces in February. By April, Japan was in full control of Southeast Asia and landed on the north side of New Guinea, threatening the Australian outpost of Port Moresby.

In Europe Britain remained unconquered. However night air attacks and German U-Boats were threatening to cut off supplies. Until now the British forces had an upper hand in North Africa. But here also the situation got worse when field marshal Erwin Rommel's Italian-German armies broke the British defenses and pursued them eastward. On the Russian front the German army still dictated the offensive although it had suffered 800,000 casualties. Most of the forward elements of the Soviet army had been destroyed. In Kiev pocket alone, 650,000 Russian troops had been taken prisoners. The best and most hopeful sign for the allies was the harnessing of US industry for the war efforts. All type of war material was flowing to every theater of war. This continued productivity proved to be the most important factor in the victory of the allies.

By May 1942 things were finally going well for the allies. The advance of the Desert Fox Rommel had been stopped in Africa. At Coral Sea naval base in the pacific, the May 7-May 8 standoff had sent the Japanese back and avoided any threat to Australia. At the Midway Base attack of June 4, Japan had lost 4 aircraft carriers. This was an irreparable loss to the Japanese army. At Goudal Canal the Japanese also tasted defeat. But the allies too had to face bitter defeats on the eastern front. General Douglas MacArthur was ordered to leave the embattled Philippians in the middle of March 1942 and on April 9 the US suffered the worst defeat in military history when 76,000 American and Pilipino troops on the Baton Peninsula surrendered. The POWs were ordered to March 65 miles to a prison camp. It was called 'Death March' as some 10,000 died on the way and 15,000 soon after in the camp from disease, wounds, and exhaustion. To raise the moral of the allies, FDR ordered the bombing of Tokyo. On April 18, Lieutenant Colonel James Doolittle led 16 B25 Bombers off the 'USS Hornet' and they bombed several Japanese cities including Tokyo.

A shame for humanity

204,000 Jews of Lodz, Poland were exterminated. Boys and girls under 10 were forced out of their houses and lined up on Lodz streets. Elderly women were rounded along their children. All were marched to the railway depot, herded into freight cars, and taken to Chelmno. There they were bathed, made to enter sealed trucks, and gassed to death with exhaust fumes. Similarly in Mizocz, Ukraine in October, 1,700 Jewish women were forced to become naked and taken to a ravine south of Rovno. There they were shot. Such heinous crimes against humanity were committed by the Nazis everywhere they went.

The end of 1942 sees the tides turning

The desert war in Africa was coming to an end. From Malta, a small island in the Mediterranean, the base for British subs and aircrafts, the British force s were harassing German supply lines. American ground forces invaded Algeria on November 8. It was called Operation Torch. Three days later the Vicky French agreed to cease fire and turned their guns on the Axis powers. Americans headed for Tunis in hopes of finishing the Germans fast. It took six months.

In Stalingrad the end game started.

In November the Red Army had completed its surprise encirclement of 300,000 Nazi troops with Germany's sixth army in its bear grip. The Red army pounced upon German positions with rocket fire. The Nazis had no supplies whereas fresh Russian reserves steamed into the battered city to replace the weary and wounded. The Germans had 20,000 casualties.

1943

The arrival of 1943 defiantly tilted the war in favor of the allies. In the Pacific Ocean the Japanese had been forced out of Cape Esperance, the northwest tip of the Guadcanal. The six-month battle had caused the death of at least 30,000 Japanese and 7,000 allied forces. Nine months later, on the Tarawa Atoll, about 1,000 US Marines and 4,700 Japanese were killed in just four days. The year began and ended with some of the most wrenching and hardest fought battles of the Pacific war. Generals like Dwight D. Eisenhower, Bradley, MacArthur, and Halsey had presented a well-knit unit and worked with full cooperation and understanding. In the Pacific Japan was dependent on the import of raw materials and fuel from its Asian empire to its home islands. By Mid-1943 the sinking of its ships by the US submarines had begun to interfere seriously with Japan's much needed vital imports. By the end of 1944 about half of Japan's fleet and 2/3 of its tankers had been sun. In support of Gilbert's, the fast carriers demonstrated their ability to take on Japanese airbases and neutralized them.

By the end of 1942 the Wehrinacht (the German army) had been encircled in Stalingrad. Hitler however had forbidden them to surrender. Faced with choice between quick death in combat and slow starvation with ultimate surrender, General Friedrich Von Paulus surrendered. This was the first victory of the Russian army in the New Year. In England Adolf Hess, Hitler's trusted lieutenant landed by parachute alone to talk about peace. He was taken prisoner. American and British Bombers were attacking German cities and centers of production in occupied Europe. Berlin raids continued for four months and 1.5 million residents were left homeless. In May Polish Jews revolted in Warsaw but were suppressed. 60,000 of them were killed or shipped to concentration camps. The massacre of Jews and Gypsies continued. In the USA factories were running at full swing. On vacant plots people were growing vegetables and other crops to make goods for the war shortages.

In North Africa General Rommel and his army had retreated to Tunisia to regroup with other German divisions. And it did. But for reasons unknown he withdrew to the south where he was defeated at the hands of British forces. Rommel flew to Berlin to ask Hitler to pull out of North Africa. But Hitler assigned him the duty defending Berlin. Trapped between allied armies, Axis forces in Tunisia ran out or fuel, ammunition, and food. To comply with Hitler's orders to fight to the last bullet, General Jurgen Von Arnim, Rommel's successor, pointed seven remaining tanks at an out of range target and told the gunners to fire until empty. Then he ordered all equipment burned and surrendered with 275,000 men in mid-May.

Operating in highly effective packs, Nazi submarines destroyed North American ships at will. Then British cryptographers cracked Enigma, the code used by the German military. The allies began rerouting conveys and finding and attacking submarines with long range planes. Of 39,000 German submariners, 33,000 were either killed or taken prisoner. By mid-1943 the Germans had lost the battle on the Atlantic.

Fall of Italy and Mussolini

The allies were not yet ready to invade France. The USA agreed to open a second front by taking Sicily. It was the largest amphibian assault in history. Fighting was fierce and not sporadic. Sicily was meant to be the platform for further action in the Mediterranean. The British troops joined General Patton's seventh army in conquering the big army in 38 days. The fall of Sicily was complicated by the country's arrest by Mussolini and its withdrawal from the Axis. Nazis who occupied much of Italy resolved to fight. Around Naples, Germans and Americans were locked in furious combat. Other allied forces were advancing in the south. On Corsica, local riflemen joined the ally forces. Hitler sent commandoes to rescue the civvies clad Mussolini from a ski lodge. He became the puppet leader of the Italian provinces still occupied by the Germans. After the fall of those provinces as well, the once powerful dictator was captured again by partisans two years later. Along with his mistress he was brutally shot dead.

1944

By 1944 million had already died and millions more were soon to die. The point of balance that had been reached was rapidly tipping largely in the ally's favor. In March, the Japanese would attempt an invasion of India from Burma. It was defeated by the 14th army composed of British and Indian troops. In the Pacific Islands the Japanese were on the defensive everywhere. In Europe Germany had lost its capacity to threaten the survival of its opponents. At sea the U-Boats had been defeated. On land the Red Army was on the offensive. In the air the Luftwaffe had been reduced to a home defense force.

Britain and America had already agreed at the Trident Conference in May of 1943 to launch a cross channel invasion in 1944. On June 6 an armada of 400 ships and 13,000 aircrafts landed 180,000 troops on the beaches of Normandy in France. The Germans were taken aback by this counterattack. By June 12 the bridgeheads had been consolidated and the allies began to push in. On June 25 the Americans broke in and on August they encircled the German army with British aid at the town of Falaise. The survivors fled across the Seine with the allies in hot pursuit. Paris was liberated was liberated on August 25, Brussels on September 3. On August 15 a Franco-American force landed in the south of France. By October the Germans were defending their own western borders.

In the east the Red Army had opened a major offensive. It resulted in the destruction of Army Group Center and led to an advance to Warsaw. The disaster of June in the west and east triggered a military revolt in Germany. On July 20 a bomb exploded under Hitler's conference table. Luckily, he survived unhurt to take terrible reprisals. General Rommel was implicated in this conspiracy and was ordered to take poison, which he did. In September Finland, Bulgaria and Romania fell to the Red Army. German troops evacuated Greece and Yugoslavia. By December most of Europe had been liberated. The allies were now able to attack Germany itself.

On the two major oceanic fronts- General McArthur in the southwest pacific and General Nimitz in the Central Pacific

Huge naval, ground and air forces were preparing to advance. In January the offensive began with the capture of Marshal Island. The offenses provoked Japan into counter offenses that resulted in the decisive Battle of the Philippine Sea of June 19-20. Admiral Ozawa, with most of Japan's surviving carriers and naval aircrafts, was devastated by Admiral Spruance's fifth fleet. Ozawa lost three carriers and, in the Great Marianas Turkey Shoot, almost 400 irreplaceable vessels. Bolstered by this success, the recapture plan of the Philippians started. Island landings began on the island of Leyte on October 20. Four major surface engagements, largely fought in the narrow waters of the Philippine archipelago, resulted in the loss of four more Japanese carriers, three battleships, 10 cruisers and 500 aircrafts.

By December, it appeared that Germany and Japan were on the brink of defeat. Their desperation led to last ditch offensives. On December 16 Hitler launched a surprise offensive against the Americans in Ardennes, the Battle of the Bulge in Belgium and Luxembourg. One Panzer group encircled Bastogne. The Americans held on to it and the allied forces made a counterattack from north and south. The bulge was slowly flattened out. The allies suffered 77,000 casualties, of which 19,000 were American.

Meanwhile the sufferings of noncombatants-Holland, Greece, the Balkans, and East Europe- increased due to shortages, hunger, winter, civil war, and depredations of the occupying armies. In the concentration camps the business of systematic cruelty, that is extermination, went on. Although Germans had lost 1.2 million soldiers their propaganda minister Joseph Goebbels was trumpeting victories on all fronts. Another important leader Himmler was also on the rampage.

1945

As 1945 opened, victory for the allies in Europe was assured. Only Hitler's iron control over the German people caused the war to drag on for four months. General Dwight D. Eisenhower, the supreme commander of the allied forces, set the tone for the final assault. Facing a certain defeat and dishonor, Adolf Hitler and his love Eva Braun committed suicide in a Berlin Bunker. He we succeeded by Admiral Karl Doenitz. The Red Army from the east had entered Berlin. In the early hours of May 7 the German high command, General Jodl and Admiral Friedberg, signed an instrument of surrender in a Red school house in Reims, France. General Eisenhower then scribed a telegram to the combined chief of staff: The mission of this allied force was fulfilled at 0241 local time, May 7, 1945.

A cruel end to a bloody war

The War in Europe had ended but dragged on wearily, drearily in the east. Japan was still fighting. In June the fifth marine amphibious corps landed on the eight square mile of Iwo Jima to begin a bombing campaign against Japan. The series of attacks resulted in some 260,000 civilian deaths and 9 million people left homeless. But Japanese determination to fight did not diminish. Finally the US President Truman, British Prime Minister Attley and Marshal Chiang Kai Shek, the new leaders of allies (death of FDR resulting in the succession of Vice President Truman, British Prime Minister Winston Churchill's party defeated by the Electorates) took the decision to drop the Atom bomb. The first bomb based on Uranium was dropped on Hiroshima on August 6, 1945. It left 94,000 civilians dead or mutilated. On August 9 another Atom bomb, based on Plutonium, was dropped on Nagasaki causing far greater loss of life and property. Such a difference between weapons compelled Japan to surrender. Three weeks later, on September 2, 1945, on the deck of the battleship Missouri Japanese foreign minister Momoru Shingemitsu signed the surrender document in a formal function preceded over by General Douglas McArthur. With this the Second World War officially came to an end.

Aftermath

Destruction in World War II was greater than the world had ever known. While most of the Democratic nations had not been conquered, they suffered greatly, Russia chief among them. The rest of the allied countries suffered huge losses in man, material, and property. In total almost 30 million people lost their lives and 80 million were left homeless. The cream of European youth was lost. These countries became so poor that starvation, unemployment, disease, and destruction hovered around. The imperial powers Britain and France became very weak. It was impossible for them to hold onto their empires for a long period. They had to dismember their empires in the next 10-15 years. In this vast ocean of destruction only the USA appeared as an island of peace and prosperity. The USA's Marshall Plan undertook the long regeneration of Europe. America became the world leader and was given the title of 'World Police'. To stop any further wars, the United Nations Organization was set up, this time with the active support and help of the USA in New York. Soon the USSR regained its power and started competing with the USA in all fields. These two power blocks- The USA leading Britain, France, and Western Europe, Japan was up against the USSR, which respectfully led East European countries. Within a few years of war, China came under Communist rule soon to become a center of great Communist power. Thus mankind entered a new kind of war: The Cold War, which continued for almost 50 years.

Germany was dismembered into western and eastern parts, controlled by the Western and the Communist blocks. Berlin, the Capital city of Germany, was also partitioned along the same line. A wall was erected signifying its split. Germany was not allowed to militarize itself. A body under the UNO was instructed to keep strict watch over the country. Japan had also suffered a lot. It joined the Americas. It was also forbidden to raise an army of magnitude.

Although the war has ended and UNO formed, the permanent peace is still elusive. New hotbeds for the renewal of war have appeared in the form of the Middle East, Africa, Afghanistan, Pakistan, Palestine, Sudan, and Somalia. A third dimension in the form of terrorism, especially by religious fanatics, has also been added to the already complicated situation of world peace. Let us hope good sense prevails and there will be no future wars of these dimensions.

A Letter About The Author

Determination is not deciding to escape a bottomless pit; it is pulling oneself out of the pit, pushing aside the thoughts of failure and ignoring the pain in the arms; it is looking past the stinging sensation of sweat and direct sunlight in the eyes. It is about using all of one's strength to pull into safety, and then reaching back into the fray to help others. Much is the same way; my grandfather was determined to crawl out of the pit dug for him. He made his life away from home, starting over many a time in new cities and in different parts of the world. I admire each of the different stages in my grandfather's life, each stage influencing me in some way or the other. A true world traveler, my grandfather helped make the life of his siblings as an early father. He has influenced me in many ways, some describable, most indescribable.

My grandfather, Mr. Bhagwat Sharan Goyal, was born on August 28, 1938. He is the second child of seven. His father, my great grandfather, set up a dry fruits business in Mathura, the town where Lord Krishna (an Indian god) was born. As time wore on, my great grandfather became the biggest dry fruit merchant in Mathura. From an early age, my grandfather was interested in studies and books; he was often found perched atop a box, telling a group of children about the stories he read. The crowd came to favor the story of the courageous Hindu emperor Hemu of Delhi, who stood against Akbar, the most famous Mughal king and nearly defeated Akbar in the second battle of Panipat during 1556. When an arrow hit Hemu's left eye, it proved fatal, and consequently India was lost to the Mughals. From then, Hemu's family disappeared to save themselves. My grandfather would never tire of telling this story, as he felt proud upon recounting the famous tales of his ancestors. This was the carefree stage of my grandfather's life. His fascination with reading has rubbed off onto me; it was he who introduced me to the pleasures of reading.

'Pran jaye, par vachan naa jaaye'. This famous Indian saying translates to 'one's life may go, but one's promise will not'. People used to live by these types of sayings in the olden days, my family no exception. It was on these principles that my great- grandfather set up his business; it was on these principles that his business died. As a rich man, my great-grandfather was very fond of dealing in stocks. One day, he went too far, and lost everything on mere words. In one smooth moment, my great-grandfather lost everything he owned, including his sanity. With a mentally unstable father and four other siblings to feed, my grandfather became the male of the household. The failing of my great-grandfather's health ushered in my grandfather's hectic stage. With the burden of responsibility thrust upon him, my grandfather matured before his time; he moved to the city with his elder brother, and began working. He would go to college in the morning, give tuitions till late evening, and study till the wee hours of the morning. My grandfather would send his entire salary home, to support his family; he put his four younger siblings through school and college with his own salary. My grandfather chose to live in humble conditions but made sure not let his siblings suffer. He procured a double post graduate degree, in English and Political Science, and went on to become a PHD in International Relations. It was then that my grandfather and his brother became teachers, the tuitions they administered as teenagers supplying them the needed experience. Taking the role of a father, my grandfather got all his younger siblings married, negotiating the deals of marriage. These were the younger, hectic days of my grandfather's life. What should have been his last carefree days became the first days of a long life of hard work and struggle. This hard work he easily smiled away is what I admire most about my grandfather. My grandfather took on tensions far older than he was yet was determined to provide for his family as any father normally would. Following his hectic days, my grandfather entered his world traveler stage, and more specifically, his African days.

In a struggle to catch up with the world, the African government announced an invitation throughout the world inviting teachers and educators into their continent. Following this announcement, my grandfather emigrated to Tanga, Tanzania, in 1969, on deputation from the government of India, which he served till retirement. Taking up his teaching job in Tanga, my grandfather raised two children and quickly became friends with his neighbors. He took his job meticulously and took his job quite seriously. He received an award for being a distinguished teacher, as he gave one of the biggest gifts possible to the African people: education. Added to the award, my grandfather was promoted to Educational advisor, a rank higher than dean or principal. Apart from his strenuous work and advising, he did not forget his brotherly duties. Love knows no bounds; even 1000 miles away, he sent money to support his family in India. Despite the difficulty of his job, my grandfather never forgot about his family and friends. He would take weekly excursions with his loved ones around Africa, developing his love for exploration through his explorations of the 'dark continent'. It was on one of these trips when my grandfather visited the Serengeti game park, the greatest and most spectacular game park in the world. On this trip, my grandfather drove a civilian car into the park. He traversed dirt paths, in search of lions, to impress his family. Through a twist of fate, the car became stuck in a mud hole. Using ingenuity, he jacked the car wheel high, and made a stone base on the hole where the wheel was stuck. The entire trip was filled in fear, as wild animals were abundant in that area, and the day wore on into night, signaling dinnertime. Eventually, he found the main road, and went back to the hotel with his family. My mother recalls that during the entire time, he wore an impassive face, and never spoke with a worried tone.

My grandfather would tell me that in Tanzania, he treated his neighbors with respect, and turned them into his second family. Whenever my grandfather toured Africa, he stayed with friends and acquaintances. If he had not made these friends beforehand, he would never have been able to travel across Africa and show his family a good time. My grandfather's ease of words has taught me that having friends and developing contacts leads to a happier and easier life.

In 1977, my grandfather returned to India with his family, bidding farewell to his friends and previous school. As an acclaimed professor, he rose to the ranks of Principal teaching job in the government institution of Delhi., and began once again living with his brothers and sister. By 1977, my grandfather had traveled the world; he had been to Spain, Morocco, Kenya, Uganda, Ethiopia, Egypt, Syria, Zanzibar, Lebanon, Iraq, Iran, France, England, Germany, Bavaria, and Japan. Through chaperoning school trips and his own explorations, my grandfather traveled across India as well. Now, my grandfather entered his retired phase. He was entering his forties and had made sufficient money to provide for his children. So, he decided to take it easy, and enjoy his life. Today, my grandfather spends his time between visiting his children in America and India. He spends his days in between time with his children and grandchildren. There is no man quite like my grandfather, and I am sure there will be none ever again.

Gaurav Jain, 2nd grandson

9 798885 910514

Printed by Libri Plureos GmbH in Hamburg,
Germany